STATE STRUCTURE AND GENOCIDE

Andrew Kolin

University Press of America,® Inc.
Lanham · Boulder · New York · Toronto · Plymouth, UK

♾™ The paper used in this publication meets the minimum
requirements of American National Standard for Information
Sciences—Permanence of Paper for Printed Library Materials,
ANSI Z39.48—1984

Contents

Introduction

Over the course of human history, countless millions have died, the victims of genocide. While scholars disagree as to how to define genocide, there is widespread agreement regarding who is the institutional perpetrator—the state—according to Chalk and Jonassohn in *The History and Sociology of Genocide*; Helen Fein in *Genocide: A Sociological Perspective*; Eric Weitz in *A Century of Genocide*; Leo Kuper in *Genocide*; Benjamin Valentino in *Final Solutions*; Robert Melson in *Revolution and Genocide*; William Rubenstein in *Genocide*; Alex Alvarez in *Governments, Citizens and Genocide*; Martin Shaw in *War and Genocide*; Irving Louis Horowitz in *Taking Lives: Genocide and State Power* as well as the articles of Isidor Walliman and Michael Dobkowki, to name a few.

For all their references to the state, none of these scholars examine the function of state as the production and reproduction of violence in terms of how the state functions. Omitted is any detailed discussion concerning the structural transformation of the state. With the exception of Holocaust scholars,[1] the idea of the formation of a specialized state mobilized by ideology to unleash extreme violence is lacking in the literature on genocide. What is also omitted from much of the literature is the idea that the roots of genocide lie in the pre-genocidal state, in the ways in which violence is woven into the social fabric, which makes the line between pre- and genocidal stages a rather thin one.

I offer yet another definition of genocide, one which takes into account the nature of the state. By analyzing how the state functions, it is possible to gain a greater understanding of why genocides occur. This takes us to the starting point, to trace the origins of the state. From there, we can examine what motivates state action. In so doing, a case can be made that states are predisposed to commit genocide.

Beginning with a state's point of origin, its power is derived from force and violence. So from the beginning, states are driven to exercise control over territory through coercion. Keep in mind that this motive is built into the structural functioning of states. Over time, the state's institutional drive to justify its actions rests on its perceived right to employ a monopoly of force and violence against those who threaten its interests. Ancient genocides were motivated by the state's attempt to establish an external claim to use violence in order to control new territory. Modern genocides are often motivated by fear of an internal threat to the state's power to control its populace. If there is a consistent link between ancient and modern genocides, it is the structural transformation of the state when the state becomes the practitioner of genocide. It is a structural transformation in the sense that the state adds on a specialized branch whose main function is to promote genocidal practices.

Ancient genocides, while they are the result of a change within the state, are non-ideological. Modern genocides lead to a structural transformation of the state, motivated by an ideology of hatred against the victimized group. The concept employed to explain this structural transformation of the state is borrowed from Ernst Fraenkel, who described the Nazi state as a "dual state." So what we have by way of a definition of genocide is not only the formation of a dual state, but also the violence used to produce and reproduce the state. Genocide is then defined as the state's use of extraordinary violence aimed at the victims.

Another aspect of this definition of genocide is the transformation of society. The social roots of genocidal practices are developed in pre-genocidal societies in terms of two related aspects, the creation of would-be bystanders and the production of violence as a "normalized" part of the social fabric. The essential group that makes genocide possible is not made up of state elites, but rather the majority of the populace that accepts the fate of the victims. In other words, understanding genocide as a societal process means taking a look at the social psychology of how the majority of people are turned into bystanders. Over time, by creating a culture of violence, nations are predisposed to accept violence as commonplace. A crisis of internal/external origin accelerates this ideology of violence, which infiltrates and eventually overdetermines the function of society and the state. In so doing, a police state is formed, which precedes the eventual formation of a dual state. With the victims identified as the source of the crisis, that part of the state specialized to mobilize using ideology will unleash extraordinary violence at the victims. The outcome raises the ultimate question for not only understanding genocide, but what to do about the power of the state?

Notes

1. These include Raul Hilberg in *The Destruction of the European Jews,* Ernst Fraenkel in *The Dual State* and Franz Neumann in *Behemoth.*

Chapter 1

The Origins of State Power

Tracing the historical and structural roots of genocidal practices requires an understanding of the origins of the state. Since any definition of genocide involves the extraordinary use of state power to destroy unarmed groups, tracing the historical origins of how states form and use that coercive might will tell us much about the structural foundations of genocide. States are a social creation, arising out of the need to organize social relations in a given territory. This key aspect of state formation was preceded by the chaotic quest during the Paleolithic period when hunters and gatherers in their search to acquire the means of subsistence were constantly on the move. At the same time, the main problem was how to construct a social process for making decisions so as to allocate resources and manpower.

In order to maximize the search for food and to maintain group cooperation, a representative was chosen in whom the authority of the group was vested. Over time, with the acquisition of more consistent means of subsistence, human populations grew. As villages formed, so did the need for simple chieftains to represent them. As these villages grew in number, they began to impinge on each other, resulting in warfare. The chief's power rested on waging and winning wars against neighboring tribes. Along with the formation of early states, came the first appearance of an agricultural surplus and expanding populations, necessitating the need for more land, which in turn, resulted in warfare. As a result, the early state was a product of a combination of factors including population growth, war, the possibility of war and conquest. What emerges as the fundamental feature of states over time is their control over the use of coercive measures. The employment of military might as the promoter and protector of the state from internal and/or external threats becomes a permanent aspect of the state.

The institutional foundations of state power are determined by the state's function as a war-making machine. With the formation of nation-states, the preoccupation was to exercise coercive control over territory through the military. States were designed to operate by coercion, whether one speaks of city-states, theocracies, or empires. Furthermore, the state maintains a right to employ a monopoly on the use of force so as to insure compliance with state mandates.

Each state that formed was usually competing with other states forming at the same time. The inevitable outcome was warfare with the driving force the acquisition of territory, which required the state to exercise the right to use a monopoly of force in order to maintain control. Relations between states took on this competitive fight for control of territory, an ongoing preparation for, and actual participation in, warfare. Therefore, built into the structure of states is a vested interest in maintaining coercion in order to fight wars. If warfare has any purpose for the state, it is to extend the state's control over territory and as a result, enlarge state power. That quest for expanding power makes warfare and the preparation for it self-perpetuating in that states must use it to acquire resources, land, supplies and men, thus making coercion a permanent feature of state function.

Over time, regardless of the form the state takes, the ultimate support and maintenance of the state is through violence. Throughout recorded history, case study after case study indicates a willingness by states to extend their territorial control through warmaking. "Between 700 and 1000 AD, Western chronicles scarcely mention a year without hostilities somewhere. From the twelfth to the sixteenth centuries, France experienced a war from 47 to 77 years in a hundred; England from 48 to 82 years in a hundred; and the states that came to be Spain from 47 to 92 years in a hundred."[1]

When states seek to expand their territorial control, the interests of the military and the state are the same. The military functions as the external coercive arm in service of the state: "The military function is performed by a public, bureaucratized profession expert in the management of violence and responsible for the military security of the state."[2] In other words, the military serves the express interest of the state, which is territorial expansion and use of state power to achieve that end. The historical pattern is that as states were formed, they developed a military in service of the state's aims. It is in the interest of state power that the state manufacture and support the ideological foundations of militarism. In essence, militarism can be understood as "a . . . preponderance of the military in the state. . . ."[3] So militarism as state ideology fits in well with the state's interest in enlargement of state power, which is accomplished by extending state violence through military intervention. The state's relentless hunger for territory serves to promote militarism. New territory acquired by military conquest is accomplished through the coercive arm of the state, the military. The disturbing implication is that this militaristic policy of land grabbing by conquest clearly places the state outside the boundaries of law in that once a state wages war, there is an absence of restraint by the conquerors. Without warfare, the states could not have expanded their territories. The fact is, early states had militarism as their guiding principle, in which the standing armies were used to expand the state and warfare was a chronic occurrence.

Warmaking serves to confront and defeat the state's external rivals. So while warmaking is the productive aspect of state formation, the reproductive aspect is not just to establish the state through warmaking, but to make war essential to the state's continued existence. Ultimately, the power a state has is measured by its quantitative control over territory. In addition, states define themselves in terms of the control they exercise over a territorially identified people.

The preceding discussion touches upon the overall theory of the state and not the nation-state, which was, by and large, a product of the nineteenth century. Prior to the nineteenth century, states did not represent nations, they served other interests, religious or hereditary rulers, such as the king, who personified the state. Any legal disputes were the king's; any and all territorial conflicts were the king's. Pre-modern states were engaged in chronic warfare in an effort to define set territory: "Fixed and limited territorial boundaries are a relatively recent invention. Throughout most of human history, the territorial base of political jurisdictions was at best fluid."[4] It would not be until the nineteenth century with the formation of nation-states that many of the Western European states would have in place well-established national borders. The formation and continued existence of pre-modern states meant that war served a two-fold end, to expand and regulate the coercive might a state could have over another state; it also served to concentrate power in a few hands. Each tendency was mutually reinforcing. War-making united and connected the interests of the state and society to the extent that militarism and patriotism had the effect of creating an acceptance of a culture of violence. Chronic warfare against perceived enemies or threats can function to prop up support for the state, to connect the fate of the people to state policy.

Whereas nineteenth century states combine two principles of rule, one representing the interests of the elites and the other representing the interests of the modern nation-state, the pre-modern state was driven by a relentless quest to acquire territory at all costs in contrast to the modern nation-state, established with more fixed territorial boundaries. In both cases, the state maintains a coercive monopoly and the right to use force and violence to extend its power by warfare. Whether one speaks of city-states, feudal states or empires, these traditional states share one feature, separating them from the modern nation-state, an effort to extend their claims to formal control over the means of violence outside of their national borders. Modern nation-states also have been successful in extending their control over the means of violence elsewhere, despite national boundaries. Modern and pre-modern states do share important common features, such as the need to maintain order in the face of any and all threats to the state, internal or external. Another important function is the myriad of activities, which connect the state to society be it the maintenance of infrastructure or provision of services through taxation. This includes creation and recreation of supports for state power, such as police and the military and state monies that support a range of cultural activities, which fall under the scope of leisure and sporting events. These are the motives that determine how the state functions and that make up the structure of the state. What needs to be discussed are the effects of the state's motives and actions. When the combination of the driving forces and the end results of state power are taken into account, the conclusion reached is that states are genocidal due to how they function. States commit genocide in order to maintain their monopoly over the use of force and violence. This crucial function of the state and how it changes over time can point to the motives behind the genocidal practices of states.

One can make a distinction as to how this operates in pre-modern and modern states. The distinction is the difference between internal and external uses of the state's monopoly on force and violence. What appears to be a driving force behind the genocidal practices of states is either a threat or crisis over how the state employs its monopoly. The waging of war against perceived external and internal enemies (the victims) is a manifestation of the state seeking total domination, complete unchallenged control of its coercive authority.

Genocides in the ancient world were carried out by states motivated by an effort to impose on other states domination of their control of force and violence. Genocide is the end result of resistance to the ancient state's efforts to impose control. The state employs force to settle the question of external boundaries not yet under the control of the state. Turning one's attention to modern genocides, in particular, those which are the product of nation-states, there is a different motive: modern genocides are the result of states waging wars in order to enforce their monopoly of force and violence against perceived internal threats. While on the one hand, ancient genocides are the outcome of states seeking to use force to control territory, on the other hand, modern genocides are the product of states which seek to consolidate control inside their borders. In the case studies, one finds evidence in support of how the state seeks to promote and protect its monopoly over violence by what has been referred to as the creation of a "dual state." This term was used by Ernest Fraenkel to describe the Nazi state, but it also can be used to explain the structure of states committing genocide. In the case studies, one finds a recurring trend, that is, states committing genocide are structurally divided into two parts, one is committed to the normal reproductive activities of the state while the other is created to perform genocide.

Notes

1. J.A. Tainter, "Evolutionary Consequences of War" in *Effects of War on Society,* G. Augenda, ed. (New York: Boydell Press, 1992) p. 107

2. Samuel Huntington, *The Soldier and the State* (New York: Vintage Books, 1964) p. 61

3. Eric Carlson, *Militarism* (Vermont: Aghate Publishing) 2001, p. 11

4. Kalevi Holsti, *The State, War and the State of War* (UK: Cambridge University

Chapter 2
Pre-modern States and Motives for Genocide

Two examples, one from ancient Greece, one from ancient Rome, serve to illustrate how genocidal practices unfold in response to the imposition of power by one state upon another. Genocide was the end result in both Melos and Carthage, when one state resisted another's claim that it held a monopoly of force over it. Athens organized the Greek city-states into the Delian League, a move that eventually repelled the Persians. With the defeat of the Persians, Athens wanted to not only hold onto its power, but also expand it. Athens faced competition from Sparta and the Peloponesian League. The Athenians were pressuring the island of Melos, which was especially attractive because of its strategic location, to form an alliance. From the Greek historian Thucydides, much is known of the dialogue between the Melians and the Athenians. Melians not only resisted the Athenian demands for assistance in the Peloponesian War, they were in effect openly defying the Athenian imposition of state power. This is apparent in that part of the dialogue in which Thucydides conveys the Athenian attitude that "the stronger should rule over the weaker." Melian resistance was calling into question the power of the Athenian state. The response by Athens was to lay siege to Melos for six months followed by the wholesale slaughter of Melians and the selling of women and children into slavery. If there is a pattern, which emerges from the example of Melos, it is that states committing genocide do so when the power of their state is challenged. Another pattern, which first appears from the example of Athens and Melos, is that states use state power to attempt to stabilize territorial ambitions. Extending the power of the Athenian state was, in the heyday of the Athenian empire, viewed as a noble goal. The philosophy of the Athenian state reduced to its simplest element is centered on the idea that the Athenians, superior and free, should rule others. Warmaking for Athens and other city-states meant fighting for justice and for a just cause, against an enemy that challenged the power of a Greek state. For the ancient Greeks, "a just cause meant simply that the enemy had wronged the state."[1] Imposition of state power by Athens over Melos translated into a doctrine of genocidal warfare. Another historical pattern, all too common in the history of genocide, is the connection between war and genocide. If there is a motive for genocidal warfare, it is the state claiming a right to extend territorial control through force and violence. In effect, genocidal wars are the external expression of state power used to dominate the territory of other states.

In genocides in the ancient world, state power leading to mass killing is the product of states that are uncertain as to their control over those states they wish to dominate. This is the issue that frames the conflict between Rome and Carthage. The various twists and turns of conflict, resolution and increased tension between Rome and Carthage over time represent the rise of Roman power in contrast to the decline of Carthage. The chain of events leading to the wholesale destruction of Carthage by the Romans is an effect of an unequal power relation between them. Rome's eventual conquest and killing of the Carthiginians can be understood in terms of Rome's efforts to broaden its power and control over territory. If there is one idea which embodies the Roman state, it is that no state, group or nation should resist Roman state power. To do so ensured one's destruction. Warfare and expansion served to demonstrate the power of the Roman state to impose its authority over conquered territories. This aspect of collective killing as the means by which state power is extended externally, as in the case of Carthage, applies in other instances of states confronting a threat to their authority, as in the example of the Vendee during the French Revlution. Unlike Carthage, this threat was not external but internal. Fearing a mass uprising, the revolutionary government committed genocide against the Vendee. In the minds and actions of the Vendeans, they were on ". . .a crusade for individual liberty, the security of persons and the preservation of possessions."[2]

What the historical record also tells us is of examples where states commit to genocide as part of the process of state formation as well as an effort to cement the power of the state. What comes to mind are two examples centuries apart, the Mongols under Genghis Khan in the 13th century and the Zulu under Shaka in the 19th century. The typical motive is present in both examples, to use state power to establish a monopoly over the use of force. For the Mongols and the Zulu, genocide functions as a useful tool with which to set a terrifying example. With Khan and the Mongols in the 13th century, genocide was a useful tool in state formation. The awe-inspiring scope and scale of genocidal practices had a political end, which was to establish Khan and the Mongols as a ruling authority determined to monopolize force and violence. The end sought by the Mongols in the employment of mass killing is territorial expansion. In so doing, the Mongols were able to exert control over an ever-expanding group of people. However, their genocidal practices did not unfold as a standard policy that would always target a group for extermination, for total destruction was not always the principal aim. Wholesale killing had to be determined to be necessary, according to a well thought out set of criteria. The Mongols were masters of killing large numbers of people for the express purpose of inflicting terror to extinguish a potential threat or enemy. The killing campaigns of the Mongols were carried out either to set an example or when absolutely necessary in order to quell resistance. Prior to any military campaign, the Mongols put into place an elaborate infrastructure of roads, a communications system and a network of spies and informers in which conquest and control were intertwined. In so doing, the Mongols could then determine if extraordinary violence was necessary.

The Zulu under Shaka, in terms of their genocidal practices, were similar to the Mongols in that they were engaging in genocide in order to form a ruling authority. As a result, the Mongols were engaging in genocidal practices in order to economize violence. Mass killing for the Mongols and the Zulu was the process by which each sought to consolidate coercive might under the control of a ruling authority. At the time, the Zulu nation comprised a large number of competing tribes. The king was the leader and the embodiment of a Zulu culture, which placed ultimate value in the warrior ideal. Zulu life was dominated by the idea of the warrior in service to the king, especially in time of war. Tribes were organized for fighting. During Shaka's reign, centralization of violence and territorial acquisition blended together with genocidal implications. With a few exceptions, the military campaigns of the Zulu were successful at wiping out enemy tribes. Only tribal chiefs who agreed to become tributaries were spared. A key element of Shaka's strategy involved mass killing in order to make a vast depopulated territory, a traffic desert. Lacking food and water and observable for miles, these traffic deserts became territorial buffers under the control of Shaka. Any tribe or persons entering the traffic desert would be spotted and killed. At the heart of Shaka's campaigns were the Impi, a specially trained military arm of the Zulu. The Impi would encircle and quickly kill, using their weapon of choice, short stabbing *assegai*.

While the examples of the Mongols and the Zulus tell us that state formation is a genocidal process, mass killing also has been the result of the state fearing a loss of coercive might as in the case of the genocide of the Hereros of southwest Africa in the early twentieth century. The revolt against the German colonizers unfolded in January 1904 and ended in 1907. Out of 80,000 Hereros, only 20,000 survived. At the root of the Hereros revolt was concern over the ever-increasing land grabbing by the Germans. In particular, with the construction of a new railroad, the Hereros had come to the conclusion that their traditional way of life, so connected to the land, was threatened. Another factor in the revolt of the

Herero uprising was the blatant racism of the colonizers, serving to further justify the violence. The threat to their traditional way of life, coupled with racism and economic ruin, only needed a spark to ignite a revolt.

In Windhoek, the Germans ordered the Bondelzwarts to turn over their guns. Resistance to this order led to a violent encounter, reesulting in the deaths of three Germans. It was not long after the German military response to this incident that the Hereros staged their uprising, intending to force the Germans to vacate Hereroland. The strategy was to engage in a kind of guerrilla warfare of hit and run targeting of German infrastructure and raids of German farms. On January 12, 1904, under the charismatic leadership of Supreme Chief Samuel Hamarero, the Hereros attacked a large number of targets, especially German farms. Genocide unfolds under the leader of General Lother Von Trotha, the commander of German military forces. The Hereros, in spite of heroic efforts, could not hope to match the superior fire power of the Germans. Von Trotha distributed the infamous extermination order in October 1904, which in its details, amount to an order to exterminate all Hereros, whether armed or not. Despite early victories, it was not long before the Germans gained the upper hand. In many ways, the fate of the Hereros was sealed in the battle of Waterberg. The genocide unfolded as the Hereros, in desperation, were able to break out of the German encirclement toward the desert. It was at this point that the murderous intentions of Von Trotha became apparent. VonTrotha's two-fold policy was to murder all captured men, women and children and to trap and isolate the bulk of the armed fighters. The trapping of the Herero fighters in the desert, thereby depriving them of food and water, ensured them of a slow, painful death. Other features of the German policy were to destroy the cultural foundations of the Hereros, seize their land and disperse them into forced labor camps.

Through imperialism, the German sought to enlarge state power, allowing it to extend coercive control over external territory. The Germans' genocidal actions stemmed in large part from the fear that the German state was in the process of losing its power over territory. This motive to commit genocide is characteristic of pre-twentieth century genocides, which are determined by the state's efforts to enlarge and consolidate its power. What is lacking in pre-twentieth century genocides is the motivating ideology of intense hatred of the victims. Genocide is a matter of necessity. The victims are obstacles to state objectives.

Notes

1. Doyne Dawson, *The Origins of Warfare* (UK: Harper Collins, 1996) p. 65

2. Reynold Secher, *The Vendee: A French Genocide* (Indiana: University of Notre Dame Press, 2003) p. 249

Chapter 3

Modern State-Sponsored Genocides

In case studies of twentieth century genocides, states wage internal wars against perceived internal threats to state power. In effect, the intense ideological hatred on which twentieth century genocides are based, is motivated by the state's perception of a direct internal threat to its power. In the case of the Armenian genocide, ruling elites perceive internal and external threats, which the perpetrators believe will undermine the power of the state. These threats were manifested as the contraction of the Ottoman Empire, the pressure to address the minorities question by European nations and the rise of nationalist movements in Turkey. The path to genocide in Turkey and elsewhere in the twentieth century is clearly characterized by those elites responsible for the manifestation of state power, engaging in genocidal practices in order to hold onto power without restraint so that when all is said and done, genocide represents a violent, anti-democratic reaction.

The starting point is the loss of the Turkish state's control over its declining Ottman Empire. Czar Nicholas of Russia referred to the Ottoman Empire as the sick man of Europe. There were many reasons for the decay of the Empire. Economic competition was a threat, coming from the ". . .growing capitalistic system in the West."[1] In addition to the loss of territories in Eastern Europe, Northern Africa and the Balkans, the empire was also in the process of losing additional territory due to the rise of nationalist movements by minorities treated as second-class citizens under the Ottomans. This nationalist fever would eventually infect the Armenians who wanted to remain part of the Ottoman Empire. They sought protection of persons and property, while at the same time, their nationalist aspirations were linked to the exercise of local autonomy. In part, this nationalism was shaped by the scores of Armenian youth who traveled to Europe for exposure to European culture and schools. They returned, full of enthusiasm for cosmopolitan attitudes. This Armenian renaissance "offered a language and a set of universal values, inspired by European literalism and romanticism. . . ."[2] Voices crying for reform were heard from European powers and from those in Turkey united by the idea that the survival of the empire depended on reform. This reform movement was the driving force behind the edicts of the Tanzimat period of 1839-1876. At least on paper, it seemed that the reformist efforts were realized with the adoption of a constitution which in principle proclaimed the ideals of equality and democracy for all Ottoman subjects, including the Armenians.

The turning point in which the Turkish state felt a clear loss of power over its empire was the Turkish defeat in the Russo-Turkish war of 1877-1878. The war was fought over Russia's intervention in order to offer protection to the persecution of Christians within the empire. The defeat of Turkey contributed to the further loss of territory. The Armenians had reason to be hopeful in 1878, when Western nations became involved in negotiations of what became known as the Treaty of Berlin. In particular, the Armenians were well-aware of Article 16, which stipulated a withdrawal of Russian troops from Turkey, if Turkey agreed to implement reforms in Turkish Armenia. But it was not long before the European powers lost interest in the implementation of reforms. Overall, the provision did not contain any means of enforcement and had no effect on the ongoing persecution of the Armenians who were the victims of a host of discriminatory measures.

Nonetheless, the Armenians continued to believe that the Treaty of Berlin was a ray of hope, which created a sense of rising expectations. There was an increase in organized political activity, which included efforts to promote the implementation of reforms. It was at this time that the Sultan Abdul Hamid II spoke out against the idea of equality and instead ". . .emphasized the utmost importance of Muslim unity and superiority within the empire and pan-Islamism without."[3] Out of desperation, the Armenians became advocates of legal and illegal strategies to acquire rights and to resist tyranny, including:

> 1) lobbying on a personal basis with Ottoman authorities perceived to be influential enough by Armenians to implement the long overdue reform statements;
>
> 2) demonstrators in the state capital airing Armenian discontent with Turkish policies;
>
> 3) Seizure of the Ottoman Bank to attract the interest of the international financial magnates involved in the Ottoman state;
>
> 4) Assassination attempts on the life of Sultan Abdul Hamid II perceived to be the mastermind behind Armenian miseries; and
>
> 5) guerilla action designed to ameliorate the lot of the Armenian villages vis-a-vis Turkish-Kurdish encroachments, heavy taxation and parasitic role.[4]

Armenian efforts to change Turkish society by the formation of their first political parties in 1855-1890 also contributed to Abdul Hamid's perception that the Armenians posed a dangerous threat. An argument can be made that the starting point of the chain of events leading to the Armenian genocide was the perception by the Turkish empire that the Armenians were conspiring with forces outside Turkey to undermine the empire, an association first made by Abdul Hamid. It is no coincidence that during his reign, he was responsible for preventing the realization of Tanzimat reforms. While a vocal minority of Armenians preached resistance, armed resistance was illegal, for the Armenians did not have the right to bear arms.

With the Turkish empire resisting formal European efforts to enact reforms, and a rising nationality problem in particular, the Armenians becoming a vocal force for equality, the Turkish empire felt a threat to its ability to compel obedience. The anti-democratic character of the Turkish state intent on maintaining control would be unleashed in the pre-genocidal massacres of the Abdul Hamid regime.

Genocidal practices in the twentieth century tended to unfold in sporadic steps as at first the state unleashed extraordinary coercive might on the victim group in an effort to reassert control. When such actions proved insufficient or the state perpetrators decided more extreme measures were necessary, the planning to restructure the state to commit genocide began. In Turkey, the first tentative steps toward genocide took place in the years 1894-1896. The coercive might of the Turkish state was unleashed against the Armenians who were to be increasingly identified as an internal threat during what became known as "the Sassoun uprising" and the massacre that followed. For those Armenians advocating resistance, the message was heard by villages of the Sassoun district, who resisted the imposition of an extraordinary tax by Kurdish chiefs. The massacre that took place in Sassoun was an organized mass killing of Armenians at a time when Turkey was not officially at war. It would last for 24 days. Abdul Hamid brutally repressed the revolt, by sending in regular Turkish troops and special Hamidiye units. Hundreds of thousands of Armenians were massacred between 1894 and 1896. What characterized the 1894-1896 massacres as pre-genocidal was the presence of spontaneous, ad hoc governmental and nongovernmental violence as well as the absence of centralized planning for the purpose of committing the government to the elimination of the Armenians. A passive response by other nations provided Abdul Hamid and the Turkish state with what amounted to tacit approval for extending the massacres. The purpose of the massacres was to silence Armenian demands for change and inform Europeans that internal reform would not be forthcoming. It is significant that the areas of the massacres, Van, Vitlis, Kharput, Diarbekir and Sivas were those where the Europeans had specified that reforms should be put in place. The massacre was followed by the

Hunchakist demonstration of September 19, 1895 by the Hunchak party leaders. This party functioned as the political voice of the Armenians. The demonstration was to be a march and rally at the Subline Porte, the center of Ottoman rule.

For the Armenians, whose purpose was to deliver a petition of outrage over the Sassoun massacre and demand equal rights, this was an historical first in Ottoman history. A minority had the audacity to stand up to the Turkish state in the capital. The Turkish state promoted the use of cudgels: "These implements are described by the Austrian Military Attache, who in 1896, was an eyewitness, as sticks fitted with a piece of iron. At a signal, the mobs, who were equipped with these cudgels, were to start killing Armenians, irrespective of age and gender. . . the methods of killing involved bludgeoning the victims with blows on their heads."[5]

The massacre of Armenians would spread to the Van in response to efforts at self-defense by Armenian revolutionary groups against the attacks of Kurdish bands. Once again, the Turkish state unleashed its coercive might against the Armenian defenders: ". . .without distinction of age or gender, women and children were killed with axes, sticks, hammers and daggers as some others were burned alive."[6] Tens of thousands in outlying villages perished. Overall, massacres took place in the six Armenian provinces of central and eastern Turkey.

What must be kept in mind was that the motive for these massacres was two-fold, to reassert the power of the Turkish state and control the political agenda that is, to prevent Armenian reform. Utmost in the thoughts and actions of Abdul Hamid, was the desire to prevent all attempts to initiate reforms, which would raise the status of Armenians. However, Abdul Hamid's violent measures would not settle the Armenian question for the Turkish state. The genocidal process unfolded as a set of circumstances that set the stage for a structural transformation of the Turkish state. This structural transformation made it possible for one part of the state to employ extreme violence targeting the Armenians for annihilation. So what we have is genocide unfolding with the creation of a "dual state." This kind of state, consisting of two parts, one functioning to perform the necessary conditions for maintenance of the social order, the other part of the state newly created whose end is genocidal, targets the victims in order to destroy them.

The starting point for the dual state is the appearance of the Young Turks, one of many elements inside and outside Turkey, that resisted the tyranny of Abdul Hamid. In Geneva, Paris and other emigre centers, reformists and revolutionaries of all the Ottoman nationalities conceived programs for change and envisaged a new, progressive government for their homeland. The Congress of Ottoman liberals, which met in Paris in 1902 and again in 1907, was developing strategies to overthrow Abdul Hamid and initiate important reforms. An important segment of the domestic opposition were junior military officers and the faculty of the technical institutes, which together formed the Committee of Union and Progress, or Young Turks. They came to power with the chief intention of stopping the decline of the Ottoman Empire, and promoting ideas of equality and rights for all Ottoman peoples, including the Armenians. In the crucial years of 1908-1914, several elements would create the conditions for the genocidal practices waged against the Armenians: the authoritarian traits of the Young Turks, an attempted coup and the shifting tide of WWI.

At first the Armenians were pleased with the Young Turk rise to power. The Young Turks did something unheard of, they armed the Armenians as a means of self-protection against attacks by extremists. Dissatisfaction of other minority groups contributed to the push for independence from the empire. Most important, the empire was experiencing any state's gravest threat, the loss of territory.

In 1908, Bulgaria becomes independent and Austria carves up Bosnia and Herzegovina. Then there was the rebellion of Albanian nationalists. In 1911, the Italians took over Libya. In 1912, the Ottoman Empire lost all of its European territories. Inside Turkey, the Armenian question had not been resolved. Armenians continued to confront attacks and in 1909, there was a terrible massacre in Adana, in which 25,000 Armenians were killed. The response of the Turkish Empire is indicative of how states will engage in mass killing in order to demonstrate state power in the face of a perceived threat. The Armenians had armed themselves for the purpose of self-defense. When they agreed to disarm, the Turkish state took revenge: "Enraged by the magnitude of the losses they sustained during the first round of the conflagration, the Turks directly supported by the newly arrived army contingents, descended upon the totally disarmed and defenseless Armenians, butchering and burning them alive by the thousands."[7] At this point, there was not yet an overall policy of mass murder coordinated by the Turkish state. While the Turkish state massacred Armenians in order to counteract a social threat, growing opposition to the regime constituted an important internal threat to the Turkish state's stability. This internal threat was short-lived, while the more persistent threat was the Armenians.

With the start of WWI, the soon-to-be perpetrators would come to view the Armenians as embodying internal and external threats to the regime. Externally, the Turkish military defeats in the 1912 Balkan War clearly represented a direct threat to Turkey because ". . .the disastrous outcome of the 1912 Balkan war left the very survival of that empire in the balance. . ." [8] The perpetrators came to see the Armenians, who lived in close geographic proximity to the front prior to and during the military setbacks, as in collusion with their enemies. The loss of the Balkans was a major disaster.

"As a result of that Balkan catastrophe, Turkey had lost nearly 70% of its European population and about 85% of its European territory."[9] The timing of the Armenians, as they sought reforms, could not have been worse. The mindset within the Turkish state was, in a twisted sense, an increasing paranoia over Armenian reformism at a time when the empire was contracting.

It is no coincidence that the political elites in the government chose this time to consolidate power. A faction within the Ittihadist party staged a coup d'etat, effectively putting in place a military dictatorship. The leaders who were to become key perpetrators of genocide, Talat Pasha, Ahmend Djenal Pasha and Enver Pasha, would come to the realization that the way to rescue the Ottoman Empire was to reject in total the tolerant multi-ethnic ideology of Ottomanism and replace it with the ideology of an emerging dual state, Turkism. The genocidal practices of a dual state depend on a utopian ideology which, in this case, was Turkism. The Turkish state was in the process of creating an anti-democratic police state, acting arbitrarily without legal restraint and backed by a willingness to use extraordinary force in support of its initiatives.

> The main instrument for this radical change was the Ittihadist party, relying on its organization and hierarchy of leadership, including its covert structures. Top priority was given to the task of creating a vast network of party branches in the provinces to be directed by trusted party loyalists. They were to be entrusted with party secrets and the execution of related party directives independent from and sometimes in contradiction of officially stated policies.[10]

The result is a state within a state. Under the leadership of the state party boss Talat, this entity became known as the Special Organization. The essence of the dual state is that it is charged with emergency powers and it functions outside the bounds of the state's reproductive process. It is not an organization designed to maintain culture and support necessary social services. It is an organization designed to destroy the enemies of the state. As a part of this special organization, the police state's functions are quite clear.

> The party directorate in close cooperation with the security office of the Interior Ministry, set up in the General Directorate of Turkish Police a special department of surveillance and intelligence where secret files were compiled on Armenian clerical, political and educational leaders as well as journalists and intellectuals as warrants for future action against them.[11]

A chain of events at the start of WWI served as the regime's justification that the Armenians constituted an internal and external threat and must be annihilated. War was viewed as an opportunity for the Turkish state to expand its coercive power, acquire new territories and destroy the enemies of the state. The wholesale killing of Armenians at the start of WWI was made possible by the Turkish state's division into two parts, one of which waged a normal military war, using troops and the other, which used its destructive capabilities to wage war against Armenian civilians. These developments began to take place when in August 1914, the Ittihad created the Special Organization under Riza, Bey and Shakir, which functions as a police and paramilitary organization with total discretionary powers.

Military setbacks, especially at the Russian front, served as the initial justification to disarm those Armenians who had enlisted to fight for Turkey. By February 1915, with the allied attack on the Dardanelles, the Turkish Army appeared to be in a state of total military breakdown. It was at this time that the Turkish government took actions to render the Armenians powerless. They dismissed Armenian civil service workers and arrested party leaders, doctors and lawyers. Disarmed Armenian soldiers were taken to isolated locations and executed. The Armenians were accused of collaborating with the Russians and therefore posed a threat in a time of war.

An extermination plan was prepared in secret by the Special Organization, staffed with party loyalists, police and common criminals, financed by the Ittihad Party and supplied with weapons from the Ottoman Army. Local Ittihad party officials were given their instructions either orally or by cable. A special deportation committee centralized in the city of Constantinople was set up under the authority of the Secretary General of the Ittihad Central Committee, Midhat Shukru. Once Shukru had his orders from the Special Organization, instructions were transmitted to the local provinces. The plan was that the murder of able-bodied men would be followed by the wholesale deportation of the rest of the population. If there is a modern element to killing, it is this introduction of deportation, the goal of which is to make the victims physically disappear. The final goal would be that no Armenians would remain in Turkey. There is no doubt that the deportation of the Armenians was state policy, given the enactment of the ". . .new emergency law called the Temporary Law of Deportation. . .to order the deportation of population clusters on suspicion of espionage, treason and in military necessity."[12] It had the effect of granting authority to deport Armenians. Most Armenians deported were women and children, since most Armenian males had already been shot. But the Special Organization staged attacks on them during the deportation, butchering helpless women and children, that is, if they survived the journey by train or on foot, without food and water. Whole families by the thousands walked on foot, eventually converging on the main deportation routes leading to the Syrian desert, where they would "disappear." Convoys from all areas merged in the tiny Armenian community of Aleppo, which linked Asian Turkey to the Berlin Baghdad railway, which in turn, was used to deport Armenians who had to pay for the privilege. They worked at a relentless pace as forced laborers with little food on various construction and road projects, eventually dying from overwork and starvation. Without food or water, other deportees were sent either east toward the deserts of Mesapotamia, where they were sent from one staging area to another, or they were transferred south to Syria, perishing in concentration camps.

The Armenian genocide was the product of profound social and state crises. The road to genocide was preceded by the vanishing glory of empire, uncertainty over the future, resistance by ruling elites to reform and identification of reform with a despised minority, the Armenians. The ruling elites transformed the Turkish state so that their solution—genocide—amounted to a perverse form of social engineering. The genocide in Turkey represents a manifestation of hatred in association with an effort to enlarge the scope of state power. The genocidal intention of 1915 may be regarded as an extreme form of state structural adaptation in which the perpetrators attempted to end the state's loss of coercive control and use its right to exercise a monopoly of violence over an ever-decreasing territory. The genocidal intent of the Turkish state was to eliminate the Armenians, to leave no physical traces and to do so in secret with minimum cost.

Russia

In October 1917, an historical first took place in Russia when the Bolsheviks, representing workers, and the peasants seized power. It became apparent to Lenin and those in the Bolshevik inner circle that their conception of socialism was at odds with social conditions in Russia. Lenin was well aware of the need to create an industrial economy and that industrialization was central to the success of the revolution, the long-term goal of which was achieving socialism. But in the absence of the classic conditions needed to make the transition to socialism, the Bolsheviks had to adjust to the prevailing conditions and in so doing, made socialist ideas into socialist ideology. In other words, Russia at the time of the Bolshevik Revolution, was lacking in a mature, capitalist economy and a large working class. Instead, Russia had a pre-capitalist economy and a large peasant class. The Bolsheviks would not exist as the party of the proletariat, but as the vanguard party. The party would in incremental steps abandon the idea of representing the ideas of the masses. In the summer of 1918, in response to the Civil War, the Bolsheviks assumed a dominant role, while opposition parties, such as the Mensheviks and the Social Revolutionaries, were excluded from having a voice in policymaking. At this time, these measures, implemented as temporary, became permanent ones. Most of all, Leninism was becoming more and more anti-democratic, with the suppression of dissent extended to supporters of the revolution as well. One such example was the sailors of Kronstadt who had played a major role in the Russian revolution and who now rebelled against the Bolshevik monopoly of power, advocating a proletarian democracy. The Leninist state in the 1920s concerned itself first and foremost with the consolidation of its power. There was no clear effort to target particular segments of Soviet society as enemies of the state to be destroyed. This idea would be characteristic of the Stalinist state in the 1930s with genocide as the result. With the Stalinist state, genocide is manifested as an internal war against enemies of the state. One of the main differences between the Leninist and the Stalinist states were the policies directed at peasants.

Overall, the Leninist state approach was the gradual transformation of the peasantry, so as to modernize Russian agriculture. The indication of this more gradual aproach was the introduction of the New Economic Plan (N.E.P.). The NEP was supposed to address many problems, the transition to socialism, the relation of agriculture to industry and the peasant issue. The NEP functioned to accept market incentives in the agricultural sector in order to secure the cooperation of the peasants. This was a period of growth for small, independent family farms rooted in the village. The long-term goal of the NEP was to slowly fit the peasants into cooperative farming.

In spite of the NEP with its gradualist approach toward transforming Soviet agriculture, the Soviet state had not cemented institutional ties to Soviet society, especially in rural areas, ". . .the Bolshevik party hardly existed in the Russian countryside before the October Revolution and even for some time after that."[13] In the countryside, party organizers faced resistance from peasant political organizations, like the peasant Skhod. Local interests took priority over national interests. When party organs were present at the local level, policy was implemented primarily through personal contacts. Party officials were often controlled by local polical elites who, overall ". . .sought to act independently from Moscow."[14]

After the death of Lenin in 1924, it would take a few years before Stalin and his followers cemented control over the party state, bringing an end to the NEP and adopting instead rapid change in both agriculture and industry. In early 1928, during the so-called grain crisis, the Soviet state under the leadership of Stalin would point the finger at the Kulaks, that segment of the more well-off peasants as the cause of the crisis due to their excess profitmaking. With the Politburo adopting emergency measures, the Soviet state now took steps to organize and forcefully seize grain: " . . .the dispatch of plenipotentiaries with emergency powers and of worker's brigades, the repression and purging of authorities who were thought to be either inefficient or recalcitrant, the setting up of Troikas for organizing the collection of grain."[15] With these steps, the Soviet Union created a state within a state, applying extraordinary measures and using extreme force to achieve state ends. By the late 1920s, a dual state has been formed, the purpose of which is to consolidate the Soviet state's monopoly over the use of force against perceived resistance to the goals of the state.

The genocidal policies of Stalinism develop at first as a newly formed part of the Soviet state, determined to violently transform Russian agriculture. The perceived grain crisis by itself contributed to, but did not cause the acceleration of violent measures against the peasants. Instead, Stalin's agenda to achieve "Socialism in One Country," amounted to an extreme, misguided violent attempt to modernize, at the time, using the power of the Soviet state to increase control over the countryside and destroy peasant political autonomy.

> A law of 10 January 1928 changed the quorum rules for the village commune meeting, so that a third of the members might bind the rest. Peasants deprived of the Soviet vote were not to vote at the village meeting; whereas labourers without a household gained that right. . . This was the beginning of the end of the independence of the commune.[16]

New measures were introduced, designed to take control over what the peasants produced and how they produced it. The official justification used to accelerate emergency measures against the scapegoated Kulaks was Article 107, used to attack persons who manipulated the price of goods. The party assumed direct control for confiscating grain within a certain period of time. Forceful appropriation led to increased demands to fulfill higher and higher grain quotas. Peasants were forbidden from buying and selling grain in the open market. Local party officials increased arbitrary methods of collecting grain from the peasants: ". . .assessment was made of the grain to be supplied by each household search, confiscation and acts of brutality on the part of local officials."[17] So with de-Kulakization and collectivization, the Stalinist state was using its coercive might to seize all grain that was produced, creating conditions for genocide. In addition, the genocidal mass famine of the Ukranian peasants serve another goal of the state, which is to strengthen its control over the Ukraine, a region known for its distinct culture and strong nationalism. It was known that increasing the quotas would lead to mass starvation. Any village that failed to meet its quota was denied food. Excess grain was stored in siloes and not released to the starving peasants. Milk produced on peasants' farms

> . . . was often processed into butter, in plants not far from the villages concerned. Only officials were admitted. One reports being shown, by a gloomy manager, the butter being sliced into bars and packed in paper bearing the imprint, in English: USSR butter for export.[18]

There was no doubt that the Soviet state from top to bottom was in the process of coordinating its efforts to forcefully extract all grain from the Ukranian peasants.

Under intense pressure from Moscow, Soviet authorities in Ukraine introduced increasingly severe measures to extract the maximum quantity of grain from the peasants. Local organizations were ordered to 'take appropriate action' to ensure the immediate repayment of grain loaned to the collective farms for the previous spring sowing.[19]

State decrees in support of this forceful extraction were in place as the Ukranian peasants continued to fall behind in meeting these arbitrary quotas.

The late summer and fall witnessed a series of repressive measures. The most serious and best known was the law of August 7, 1932 on safeguarding Socialist property. The law provided for execution or ten years of imprisonment for 'pilfering' even an ear of wheat or a sugar beet root from the crop grown by peasants.[20]

The state was driven by two motives, to further the Stalinist ideology of rapid change, while seeking to make the peasants an example, through the forceful seizure of grain. In so doing, the Soviet state was justifying its perceived right to use extreme violence against the peasants.

As the entire harvest of a given collective farm was brought to a single point and placed under state control, the state would dispose of it as it pleased. Obligations to the state, as the state determined them, and to the collective farm administration had to be completely fulfilled before any produce whatsoever was distributed to those who had produced it. If the harvest fell short or merely equalled the amount demanded, the peasants received nothing and thorough searches were made of members' homes for any food that might make up for the shortfall.[21]

The grain seizures came to represent the Soviet state's internal war against the peasants. State ideological mobilization tied the central state to local state authorities to use state power to attack the peasants. What points to this goal are the decrees issued in 1932:

The decree ordered district executive committees and village Soviets:
1) To verify immediately with documentary data every collective farm's level of fulfillment of the grain procurements plan; to verify the existence of bread resources in collective farms which are lagging in the grain procurements, turning particular attention to the existence of hidden grain, especially in straw, chaff, sediments and so forth; to immediately organize the return of illegally distributed

bread and its inclusion in the grain procurements; to organize the confiscation of
bread stolen in the collective farms, above all from idlers and loafers who have
bread without working.

2) To force the tight-fisted to surrender immediately their granaries of bread and
apply them to their quotas; to demand from individual peasants the closest daily
fulfillment of the grain procurements plan; to apply immediately and resolutely
the measures outlined in the UKSSR decree of November 20, 1932 to those individual peasants who maliciously undermine the grain procurements.[22]

Further evidence of how the Soviet state during the crucial year of 1932
sought to tighten political control over the grain quotas is indicated by
Molotov's political role in the Ukraine:

... at the end of October 1932 a special commission on procurements headed by
Viacheslav Molotov, USSR head of state, arrived in Kharkiv, then the capital of
the Ukranian SSR, in order to take charge of the procurement campaign there.
Molotov remained there until January 1933, directed the procurements campaign
and supervised the work of the republic-level officials in this area.[23]

As the famine was unfolding, the Soviet state's war against the peasants
amounted to Stalin using the might of the state to tighten his control over the
state apparatus:

By taking advantage of the famine, Stalin was able to withdraw the concessions
earlier made to the Ukranians and 'solve' his Ukranian problem. In December
1932, he ordered that the 'mechanistic' implementation of Ukranization be replaced by a campaign to disperse Petliurists and other bourgeois nationalist elements in the Ukraine.[24]

At the height of the Famine, in early 1933, in addition to the visible effects of starvation, such as swollen faces, legs and stomachs, people out of
desperation, ate anything ". . .mice, rats, sparrows, ants, earthworms. They
ground up bones into flour and did the same with leather and shoe soles;
they cut up old skins and furs to make noodles of a kind and they cooked
glue."[25] People killed each other over the smallest morsel of food and canni-
balism was not uncommon. Those who could travel to railway stations were
denied access to trains. Many begged for food and died at the stations.

The genocidal policies of mass murder to achieve the objectives of
the Soviet state continued with the Gulag labor camp system. An extensive system of camps was designed to achieve rapid industrialization by
forced labor in which the conditions in many of these camps proved to
be fatal to the inmates.

An important distinction needs to be made between the pre-genocidal and genocidal periods in the labor camps. The establishments that would later under Stalin become the Gulag or the Main Administration of Corrective Labor Camps and Labor Settlements did not manifest a genocidal role during the Communist regime. Under Lenin's rule, any person or group that threatened the new Bolshevik government was confined. Prisoners were to be politically reeducated and those who responded were given additional privileges and better food. Labor was an important part of the reeducation process. As a result, there was a merging of corrective labor and corrective labor institutions as idea and practice. There were a host of police agencies, the Cheka and later on the NKUD that had control over the arrest, confinement and execution of prisoners. The Cheka was an innovative agency that set up concentration camps to house political opposition. At the end of the Civil War period, these agencies still had the power to imprison anyone:

> Administrative arrest still threatened the entire non-party population, but now at least, only four agencies could employ this measure: the Cheka, NKUD, local Soviets and the newly established Administrative Commission of Petrograd.[26]

The concentration camps under the jurisdiction of the Cheka dealt with opposition to Lenin's regime without regard to due process: "There were executions without trial and death sentences were frequently imposed upon innocent people."[27] In addition, the Cheka concentration camps made use of forced labor. Prisoners were forced to work in forests to produce lumber. The camps were not well run and the conditions inside the camps and the extreme temperatures in winter led to a high mortality rate. However, there was no relation between worker productivity and survival.

After Stalin's "Great Turning Point," in which the Soviet Union was supposed to experience rapid industrialization, the camps became genocidal, in that in order to survive, inmates had to produce in accordance with state goals. If they did not, they received less and less food and eventually starved to death. The abitrary nature of the production goals resulted in millions of deaths in order to further the goal of rapid industrialization. The clearest example of genocidal intent in service of state objectives was the labor camp complex of Kolyma, the Arctic labor mining camps. Underfed and overworked prisoners existed for the sole purpose of providing the government with gold. In essence, the Kolyma camps mass murdered through the "norm system," under which labor output at higher and higher norms was linked to food rations. As with the state structures that caused the Ukranian mass famine, the Gulag camp system was in effect a state within a state. In the case of the Soviet state, genocidal practices can be identified as the state becoming divided in function. This is the situation as one looks at the setup of the Gulag system and finds:

... many of the requirements which the government of a nation state would have
to meet. Security, healthcare, education, provision of food, political indoctrination, surveillance—all of these roles exercised by the Soviet government in national life had their Gulag equivalents organized by Gulag departments.[28]

When one considers the broad categories of groups subject to imprisonment in the Gulags, it is clear that the Gulags were part of an effort by
the Soviet state to maintain control and exercise violence against perceived
enemies of the state. By and large, the genocidal aspect of the Gulags lies
in the system of "Norm Determiners," who controlled who lived and who
died. Norm Determiners did the math, figuring out the amount of work
each detainee would have to perform in order to receive the daily ration.
The twisted dimension of the norm system is that it was ever-changing
and norms continually increased while rations did not. The overall purpose
in the long term would translate into working the inmates to death, while
denying them food. Since the authorities were well aware of what was
needed to sustain the inmates, it must be concluded that the Gulag system
was set up to produce genocide.

Notes

1. Richard Hovaninisian, "The Armenian Question 1878-1923" in *A Crime of Silence:
The Armenian Genocide* (ed) Gerald Libaridian (UK: The Zaryan Institute, 1985) p. 12

2. Stephan Astourian, "Genocidal Process: Reflections on the Armeno-Turkish Po-
larization" in *The Armenian Genocide in Perspective,* Richard Hovaninisian, ed. (New
Jersey: Transaction Press, 1986) p. 57

3. Kevork Suakian, "The Preconditions of the Armenian Turkish Case of Genocide" in *Armenian Review* Vol. 34, 1981) p. 406

4. *Ibid* p. 407

5. Vahakn Dadrian, *History of the Armenian Genocide* (UK: Berghahn Books, 1995) p. 120

6. *Ibid* p. 136

7. *Ibid* p. 183

8. *Ibid* p. 184

9. *Ibid* p. 193

10. *Ibid* p. 196

11. *Ibid* p. 197

12. *Ibid* p. 221

13. Samuel Farber, *Before Stalinism: The Rise and Fall of Soviet Democracy* (UK: Polity Press, 1990) p. 25

14. *Ibid* p. 41

15. Moshe Lewin, *The Making of the Soviet System* (New York: Norton Press, 1994) p. 97

16. Robert Conquest, *Harvest of Sorrow* (New York: Oxford Press, 1986) p. 90

17. Moshe Lewin, *Russian Peasants and Soviet Power* (Evanston: Northwestern University Press, 1968) p. 226

18. Conquest, p. 235

19. James Mace, "Genocide by Famine in Ukraine, 1932-1933" in *State Violence and Ethnicity,* Peter L. Van den Berghe, ed. (Colorado: University of Colorado Press, 1990) p. 57

20. *Ibid* p. 57

21. *Ibid* p. 58

22. *Ibid* p. 60

24. *Ibid* p. 62

25. *Conquest*, p. 244

26. Michael Jakobson, *Origins of the Gulag: Soviet Prison Correctional System 1917-1934* (Lexington: University of Kentucky Press, 1993) p. 24

27. David Dallen and Boris Nicolevsky, *Forced Labor in Soviet Russia* (New Haven: Yale University Press, 1958) pp. 157-158

28. Edwin Bacon, *The Gulag at War* (New York: New York University Press, 1994) p. 64

Chapter 4
Nazi Germany

In many ways, Nazi Germany is a classic example of how the formation of a "dual state" leads to mass murder. This dual state infused with an ideology of hatred waged both internal and external wars against the racial enemies of the Nazi state, especially Jews. It made use of extraordinary coercive force in a global effort to expand its power while engaging in an obsessive effort to destroy the Jews and other racial enemies. In large part, the roots of this dual state appeared during World War I and its aftermath, a war that began with Germany's determination to make itself a dominant world power. After it was defeated, Germany made its first genuine attempt to create a democratic system. It was the failure of the Weimar Republic that created the conditions for the dual state. From 1919-1933, there were no less than 23 governments in Germany. The streets were filled with the ranks of the discontent. The left and the right were in agreement on the need to abolish both the Versailles Treaty and the Weimar Republic.

The provisions of the Versailles Treaty struck at the heart of German national pride. The most despised provisions were those concerning Germany's territorial losses, reparations and measures designed to turn Germany into a second-rate power. In essence, the Weimar state, so much associated with the Versailles Treaty, represented to many Germans the weakness of Germany and above all, the embodiment of a weak state. While the Weimar Republic eventually succeeded in suppressing the left's attempts to overthrow the Republic, the right was growing in influence, especially a number of small, anti-Semitic organizations. Anti-Semitism was common among high-ranking military officers. There was also anti-Semitism among former soldiers who became the backbone of paramilitary orgnaizations in the 1920s, in particular the "Free Corps." At this time, Hitler was in Munich, working for military intelligence officers, who were collecting data on various political organizations. Hitler was recruited to infiltrate the small German Worker's Party, which would eventually become the National Socialist German Worker's Party or the Nazi Party.

Hitler's obsessive anti-Semitism was by this time full-blown. His hatred of the Jews determined his politics and personal views. Hitler's worldview was of an eternal struggle between two forces, the Aryan, who personified racial purity, against the Jews, the embodiment of racial pollution. On a personal level, Hitler blamed the Jews for his failure to become a respected artist and for the death of his mother at the hands of a Jewish physician. It was not long before he became the official head of the Nazi Party. By mid-1921, the party had organized its street fighters, the Storm Detachments or SA, whose ranks were filled with former members of the Free Corps.

The rising anti-democratic mood along with an economic downturn and the French occupation of the Ruhr, which led to more unrest, were for Hitler signs that Bavaria could be the spark to ignite a national revolution. The failure of the Beer Hall Putsch with Hitler's subsequent imprisonment drove home the realization for Hitler that if the Nazis were to rise to power, they could not do so by a direct violent assault against the Weimar Republic. They would have to work within constitutional or legal means. This meant the creation of a mass political party that would actively compete for votes with other political parties in Weimar Germany.

Between the years after Hitler's release from prison until the late 1920's, the Nazi Party was not taken seriously and was often the subject of ridicule. This was a period of prosperity in Germany in large part due to loans which kept the economy afloat. In the elections of May 20, 1925, the Nazi Party's numbers were unimpressive, a mere 810,000 votes out of a total of 31 million cast. The chief rival of the Nazi Party, the Social Democrats, gained over a million and a quarter votes, they polled 9 million and with their 153 seats in the Reichstag, they were the largest political party in Germany.

But with the global Depression of 1929, the political fortunes of the Nazi Party were about to change. If the Depression had any political implications, it was to create a social climate filled with desperation and with it desperate solutions. The fear and uncertainty were compounded by all the violent street battles between the left and the right. The economic picture was dire. "Thirty-three per cent of the workforce were without jobs."[1] What also was significant was the lack of relief provided by the Weimar government. "By early 1933, only nine hundred thousand among more than six million unemployed received natural insurance assistance. Certain categories of worker—in farming, fishing and forestry—were excluded altogether, as were most workers under twenty-one years of age."[2] As a result of the Depression, Nazi representation rose to 107 deputies in the July 1930 election. Parliamentary democracy was disappearing. "Each year, Parliament sat for fewer days: ninety-four in 1930; forty-two in 1931; thirteen in

1932."[3] This was followed by an ever-increasing concentration of power within the Executive branch which was governing through the use of arbitrary decrees, resulting in a goverment that functioned in the margins of rule by law. "The increasing resort to Presidential emergency decrees marginalized the legislature and unelected senior civil servants who drafted these often highly technical instruments gained in importance. Over time, this exceptional form of government, suspended between parliamentary democracy and authoritarianism came to seem normal."[4]

Also contributing to the increasing concentration of power was the alienation of popular support from the main political party, the Social Democrats, which was associated with the shortcomings of the Weimar Republic's welfare state, especially the minimal safety net provisions during the Depression. Popular support was shifting toward the Communists and the National Socialists and away from the Social Democrats. The Nazi messages of getting Germany out of the Depression, German nationalism, measured doses of anti-Semitism and the Fuhrer principal of following the leader, all combined to give the Nazis their best electoral showing in the 1932 elections, garnering 37 per cent of the vote, which translated into 230 seats in the Parliament. At the time, the internal backstabbing and power grabs within the Executive branch all contributed to setting the stage for Hitler's invitation into the collapsing Weimar state, where he would out-maneuver his rivals to eventually become Chancellor.

What remained of democracy in Germany was eliminated with the Reichstag Fire, staged by the Nazis, who alleged that it was part of a Communist attempt at a coup d'etat. The result was the "Decree of the President for the Protection of People and the State of February 28, 1933." This was an important first step in creating the political conditions necessary to concentrate political power without any legal restraints. It also was the means by which state power could be exercised without any limits, as to the application of force and violence. In essence, the decree created a police state, for it eliminated all civil liberties, such as freedom of expression, of assembly and of the press and it made the state all-powerful, suspending any limits on police powers and any notion of procedural due process.

Working in tandem with the decree of February 28th was the Enabling Act of March 24, 1933. With the Enabling Act, the concentration of power creates a quasi-legal foundation for Hitler's dictatorship, placing at its disposal the new Fuhrer principal, the absolute authority to employ without question the coercive might of the state. This marks the beginning of the pre-genocidal phase of the dual state. During its formation in the early 1930's, it will become increasingly specialized, not only in its extraordinary centralization of power within a separate part of the Nazi state but also as an instrument guided by Hitler's obsessive anti-Semitism, targeting the Jews for extermination in the early 1940's.

Several additional measures in 1933-1934 served to further consolidate the Fuhrer state and were part of the process of the establishment of
the dual state. In the spring of 1933, rival political parties were forcefully
eliminated. As of July, a law was enacted making the Nazi party the only
legal party in Germany. By August, after the death of President Hinden-
burg, the titles of President and Chancellor were merged, with Hitler as-
suming both. Ernst Rohm, the SA leader, had envisaged the SA as a functioning part of Germany's armed forces. Rohm's rivals convinced Hitler
that he posed a direct threat. In addition, the German Armed Forces were
reluctant to support Hitler without the elimination of Rohm's private army.
In June 1934, Rohm and the other leaders of the SA were executed in what
become known as the "night of the long knives."

The evolution of the dual state in particular, its police state functions,
cannot be understood apart from its ideological motivation to confront all
enemies of the regime, whether political or racial. Essential to the Nazi
dual state during the 1930s is the growth in power and scope of the SS.
Hitler realized Himmler's potential early on when they first met in the
1920s. Hitler recognized Himmler's fanatical devotion and attention to detail and awarded him with positions of increasing importance in the party
hierarchy. "In 1925, he became Deputy Gauletier of Upper-Bavaria-Sweba
in the same year Deputy Reich Propaganda chief, in 1927 Deputy Reich
Fuhrer-SS."[5] In 1929, the SS consisted of just 280 men, the bodyguards
and henchmen of the Nazi party; but under Himmler's leadership, they
could come to represent the fusion of a racist ideology backed by the most
brutal measures against political and racial opposition to the Nazi regime.
Embodying the principles of a police state, the SS was in the business
of collecting intelligence and spying, which developed under Himmler's
righthand man, Reinhard Heydrich, who became the head of the SD or SS
Security Service. Overall, the internal development of the SS in the 1930s
was a state within a state.

The state within a state is apparent when one examines the broad range
of SS functions, from the special intelligence services of the SD, which
would merge with the Gestapo, and other bureaus which would become
the RuSHA. The SS had its own fighting forces, the Totenkopfverband or
"Death Head" formations as well as the Verfugungstruppe, the General
Service SS Troops. The bureaucratic structure of leadership within the SS
provides further evidence of the SS as a state within a state:

> The Higher Organisation of the SS order was also reminiscent of that of the
> Jesuits. Ignatius Loyola, the founder of the Jesuits, organized a kind of Govern-
> ment of his order with a General at its head, advised by four assistants. Himmler
> followed the same system when he set about organizing a central compound
> structure of the SS. In place of the Jesuit General's four assistants, the Reich-

Fuhrer SS was assisted by a number of Hauptamter [Departments]; first came the
private office under Brigadefuhrer Karl Wolff, the highest SS operational staff,
re-named Personal Staff ReichFuhrer SS in 1936 and raised to Hauptamt status
in 1939; next came the SD-Hauptamt under Gruppenfuhrer Reinhard Heydrich,
the directing organization for the Security Service, third came the Rasse und
SiedLungshauptamt—Race and Resettlement office—RuSHA under Obergrup-
pefuhrer Walter Darre, who was also Reich Minister of Agriculture; fourth came
the head of the SS-Gericht [SS Court] Brigadefuhrer Paul Scharyre, responsible
for special SS jurisdiction also raised to Hauptmat status in 1939' finally, there
was the SS Hauptmat under Wittje's successor, August Heissmeyer, the administrative center for all SS units with the exception of the SD.[6]

The central role that the SS assumes during the Holocaust starting
in 1941 was the result of a number of factors. There is no doubt that
Himmler's anti-Semitism functioned as the ideological motivation to target the Jews; it is well-known that his anti-Semitism was second only
to Hitler's. However, the anti-Semitism of Hitler and Himmler cannot
fully explain the chain of events leading to the mass murder of the Jews.
One cannot overlook the structural transformation of the German state,
especially the SS reliance on extraordinary violence which was used in
service of internal and external wars against the Jews. Also not to be over-
looked is the fact that other key perpetrators such as Heydrich and Eichmann, did not possess the anti-Semitism of Hitler and Himmler. They
were dedicated state bureaucrats who ensured that the mass murders took
place with the utmost efficiency. The calculated, genocidal actions of the
Nazi state from 1941 were no doubt part of the global racial war waged
by Nazi Germany, led by Hitler but an essential part of the genocide was
the process, starting in Germany in the 1930s, in which the SS assumed
control of anti-Jewish measures. Until the SS involved itself in the Jewish question, there were no clear policies and no master plan. The rank-
and-file party members wanted to step up anti-Jewish measures but there
was no clear course of action. High-ranking party members advocated a
cautious approach in part out of concern for world opinion. Inspired by
the Minister of Propaganda Joseph Goebbels, members of the party rank
and file advocated a one-day economic boycott on April 1, 1933. But with
little enthusiasm, as many Germans were still buying items from Jewish
shops and with insurance companies providing compensation for dam-
ages, the boycott was a failure.

A more rational approach advocated by bureaucrats during what became known as the legal phase was the adoption of anti-Jewish laws.
Eventually, over 400 such laws passed, amounting to a pattern of segre-
gating Jews from Germans. The most significant part of the legal phase
was an important building block in what would become the Final Solution.

With the Nuremberg laws, which sought to define what a Jew is, racism acquired legal standing.

When the SS took a greater interest in the Jewish question, it was at first following past precedent in promoting Jewish Emigration. As early as the summer of 1934, the SS concerned itself with Jewish Emigration, issuing a seven-page report, "Situation Report—Jewish Question." Heydrich and especially Eichmann, took an interest in the emigration of Jews. Eichmann's reputation as an expert in Jewish affairs served him well when he assumed the position within the SD section II 112, regarding questions on the Jews. Eichmann advocated the mass emigration of Jews. It was in Austria that Eichmann had learned much about how to force Jews to emigrate. It was also at this time that the Nazi regime toyed with the idea of sending the Jews elsewhere such as to Madagascar, which never came to fruition. The Lublin reservation was an example of forced emigration, which had tragic consequences for those deported. The combination of the crowded transports without food or water contributed to a high mortality rate. Those who survived the journey died in large numbers at the makeshift camp due to exposure, lack of food and unsanitary conditions.

Of greater significance than the SS involvement in emigration was its takeover of the "Wild Camps" of the SA, originally intended to house and reeducate opponents of the regime. Under SS control, the camps were standardized in terms of their daily operations. During the war, the camps' purpose would shift to include the destruction of Nazi Germany's racial enemies. Starting in 1939, events inside and outside Germany would point to a shift in policy toward the Jews as well as the role that anti-Semitism would assume in relation to Germany's territorial ambitions. From 1939-1941, Nazi policy toward the Jews was undergoing a transformation in the sense that the key policy makers agreed that current policies, in particular emigration, were proving to be unworkable. This steady abandonment of past anti-Semitic practices paved the way for what would become the "Final Solution." This shift and search for alternatives to past precedent is evident in the Euthanasia program and the formation of the ghettos in Poland. These two developments are the first indications that anti-Semitic policies and territorial expansion would result in incremental mass killing.

With the conquest of Eastern and Western Europe, Nazi policymakers were moving away from expansion to concentration of Jews within the conquered territories. Poland with its estimated 3 million Jews and millions of Jews in Western Europe would present Nazi perpetrators with a dilemma. With military conquest, the Nazis had acquired more Jews. The ghettos in Eastern Europe were designed as a stop-gap measure, a temporary solution until a permanent one could be found. The Jews were for Hitler, Himmler and other anti-Semitic ideologues, an obstacle to "Lebensraum," living space, and to fulfilling the utopian ideal of a world controlled by the pure Aryan race. From 1939-1941, there was no overall plan for physically removing the Jews from sight and destroying them. Nonetheless, the functioning of the Eastern European ghettos points to an interest in slow, incremental killing of the Jews. If the ghettos had a function other than concentration of the Jews, it was that the conditions were such that Jews would die slowly from starvation and disease. In the words of Hans Frank, the head of the General Government, where Jews in Poland were concentrated, in August 1942,

> The fact that we shall be condemning 1,200,000 Jews to death by starvation should be mentioned incidentally. Of course, if the Jews do not die from starvation, it is to be hoped that anti-Jewish measures will be expedited in the future.[7]

In the Warsaw Ghetto, as of January 1941, ghetto inhabitants could expect to receive an official daily food ration of about 219 calories. In the Kovno Ghetto, inhabitants would receive a daily ration of about 750 calories. Within the Vilna Ghetto, the caloric intake was about 500 to 600 calories. What is well-documented from the diaries of ghetto residents is that without smuggling, many more would have died a lot sooner. In the Warsaw Ghetto, 80 per cent of the food, according to one account was smuggled in. After starvation, it was disease that contributed to the ever-increasing mortality of ghetto inhabitants. In part, disease was caused by severe overcrowding and poor hygiene conditions. In the Lodz Ghetto, 95 per cent of the apartments lacked toilets or running water. Without heat or proper ventilation, the ghettos were breeding grounds for disease. All the ghettos had outbreaks of typhus, spotted fever and dysentery. The wholly inadequate diet contributed to a weakening of resistance to disease. German authorities were well-aware of these conditions and made no effort to provide additional food or medical supplies to the residents. Instead, the difficult task of managing the internal conditions of the ghettos fell upon the Jewish Councils, utterly lacking in funds and essential supplies.

It is no coincidence that the appearance of the Euthanasia program coincided with the formation of the Eastern European ghettos. Both point to the evolution taking place within the Nazi state and in the minds of key perpetrators, an incorporation of incremental mass killing as functional to the goals of Nazi ideology. Both the Euthanasia program and the Nazi policies of ghettoization provide evidence of the Nazi dual state. On the one hand, the medical profession performs its normal state-related functions, supposedly according to the motto, to do no harm.

Hitler had for some time, expressed an interest in medical killing. As early as 1935, he expressed this interest to Dr. Wagner at the Nuremberg Rally. His conception of racial purity was tied to ideas of eliminating racial, physical and mental inferiors. The spark that ignited the initial medical killing program was the petition of a parent requesting the mercy killing of an infant child born blind, with one leg, with one part of one arm missing and identified as feebleminded. In early 1939, Hitler's personal physician Karl Brandt was sent by Hitler to the hospital where the child was a patient in order to verify the diagnosis. Once verification of the child's condition was made, Hitler was convinced of the need for a special state-run program of Euthanasia. Run from Hitler's Chancellory, headed by Philip Bouhler, the wholesale killing of first children and then adults identified with specific conditions was underway. The examinations amounted to nothing more than making sure the intended victim and paperwork matched; medical doctors could authorize medical killing simply by putting a plus sign in the left column of a paper form.

Hitler's authorization of medical killing appears in a document backdated from October 1939 to September to coincide with the start of the Polish campaign. The letter indicates that responsibility for the program lay in the hands of Bouhler and Dr. Brandt. The process of killing the victims illustrates the pioneering aspects of the program. Deception was its hallmark, from the so-called diagnosis to the transport and killing of the victims. In particular, the novel element of killing using carbon monoxide gas, the use of which, along with the construction of the gas chambers under the authority of the SS police official Christian Wirth, was a forerunner of the killing process in the camps. During the Euthanasia program, Jews did not have to meet the standard criteria for medical killing. If Jews were simply in a medical or psychiatric facility, they were targeted to be killed. As early as April 1940, the Reich Interior Ministry issued directives to identify and target Jews as victims of the program. It was not long after this proclamation that the gassings of Jews began, with more killings in July and August. The importance of the Euthanasia program cannot be understated, for the staff would later serve in the camps. It was during the program that there arose the new ". . . system of stealing gold teeth and bridgework from the corpses of the murdered victims. . ."[8]

Between 1939 and 1941, it became clear to the Nazis, especially Hitler, that previous attempts to solve the Jewish problem were proving to be unworkable. In early spring 1941, a radical shift in thinking was occurring. With the impending invasion of the Soviet Union, which would only add to the number of Jews under Nazi control, Nazi leaders were convinced that the Russian campaign would be a war to annihilate racial enemies. In Russia, the merging of anti-Semitism with territorial ambitions was clearly genocidal. These motivations would lead to piecemeal policies in Russia, resulting in the mass shooting of Jews. The Russian campaign unfolded as the inauguration of the Final Solution.

Once the Russian phase of the Final Solution was complete, the focus would shift from the extermination of Eastern European Jews to Western European Jews. This emphasis on a continent-wide campaign of mass killing clearly sets the Holocaust apart from other examples of genocide. The destructive machinery of the Nazi state was made possible by the extensive pre-war planning between the German Army and the SS. With the Barbarossa decree, the killing of political and racial enemies became a matter of state policy. The decree coordinated areas of responsibility for the Army and the Einsatzgruppen. In a March 26, 1941 agreement with Army Quarter Master General Edward Wagner, Heydrich, who had overall authority of the Einsatzgruppen, spelled out what would be the areas of responsibility and actions of the Einsatzgruppen near military operations and authorized the shooting of segments of the Jewish population. The purpose of these shootings was to eliminate what the Nazis identified as Commissars, those who were the disseminators of the Jewish Bolshevik view in the Red Army. By July 1941, other categories of Jews who were to be shot were added. From July 11, according to Commander of Police Regiment Center Lieutenant-Colonel Max Montna, Jewish males from the ages of 17 to 45 were to be shot. By August 15, the Einsatzgruppen were shooting Jewish women and children as well.

Heydrich had on July 17 worked out an agreement which in effect authorized the shooting of elements identified as "politically intolerable," which meant all Communists and all Jews. The killers who made up the leadership of the Einstazgruppen were drawn from the professions and were well-educated with degrees in law, architecture, medicine, theology, economics and business. The actual shooters fanned out, following the Army during the Russian campaign, supplemented by members of the Order Police, Germans who for various reasons did not qualify for duty with the regular German Army. The preserved Einsatzgruppen reports, which survived the war, document the extent of the shooting of Jews throughout Russia. Nazi perpetrators over the course of these mass shootings came to realize their inherent shortcomings. The incident that took place in mid August 1941 illustrates that Nazi perpetrators were becoming concerned over these shootings. Himmler visited Minsk to observe the shootings. Von-Denn Bach confronted Himmler after the shooting, remarking how distressed the shooters were. Himmler was concerned enough to request a search for an approach that was more distant and humane.

The importance of this incident points to another disturbing feature of the Holocaust that sets it apart from other genocides, that is, the obsession with developing the most efficient and rapid techniques with which to murder the Jews. The gas vans were developed as a means of avoiding a breakdown in the killing. The inventor of the gas van, Walter Rauff would remark on this need to deal with the psychological difficulties of the shooters: "I cannot say whether I had misgivings about the use of gas vans. What was uppermost in my mind at the time was the shootings were a great strain on the men involved and that this strain would be removed by the use of the gas vans."[9] Throughout the period when the gas vans were used, there was a clear understanding of the problems associated with them. Some problems were technical, such as how to best proceed with killing the intended victims, which Rauff described:

> Greater protection is needed for the lighting system. The grill should cover the lamps high enough to make it impossible to break the bulbs. It seems that these lamps are hardly ever turned on, so the users have suggested that they could be done away with. Experience shows, however, that when the back door is closed and it gets dark inside, the load pushes hard against the door. The reason for this is that when it becomes dark inside, the load rushes toward what little light remains. This hampers the locking of the door. [10]

Other obstacles that impaired the smooth operation of gas vans were the length of time it took to kill and the number of victims, both of which varied: "The exhaust gas killed in a quarter of an hour and a group of trucks working five times a day permitted the daily killing of 600 to 900 persons."[11] Part of this search for greater killing effectiveness is evident in the Wannsee Conference of January 20, 1942, which in essence would draw in the rest of German society and other parts of the German government to coordinate all their energies toward the Final Solution. Heydrich, placed in charge of carrying out the Final Solution, focused the conference on the overall task of making the Final Solution function as a vast bureaucratic operation. The motivating force behind mass murder in the Holocaust is an ideology of hatred, which established the creation of a district state within a state or a dual state, which has a bureaucratic commitment to use extraordinary violence to exterminate the Jews. The bureaucratic implementation of the Holocaust is clear in an examination of Eichmann and the deportation process. This massive movement of Jews from Western to Eastern Europe was in part a vast police operation. These roundups were carried out by the Gestapo, often assisted by regular local police, Order Police and the Criminal Police. Throughout Western and Eastern Europe, these roundups were made possible by earlier registration, identification of the Jews. In Eastern Europe and Russia, the goal of ghetto clearing operations, like those in Western Europe, was to deport Jews to be killed in various camps. Standardization of procedure was the key bureaucratic element in the deportation process.

The destructive machinery operated as a division of labor within the state. Eichmann's role within the Reich Main Security Office or RuSHA in IV-B4 gave Eichmann the authority to seize and deport Jews. Eichmann's bureau concerned itself with the deportation process outside of Poland. Within Poland, the deportation of Jews to their deaths in the camps fell under the authority of "Gedob." On the other hand, the Transport Ministry had the responsibility of coordinating train traffic in Europe. Working with the Transport Ministry, Eichmann's bureau would deport Jews using the railway system, or Reichbahn. The deportation of Jews took the form of a bureaucratic request for special passenger trains by the RuSHA which in practice, were death trains but this function of sending Jews to their deaths was regarded as just a matter of proper shipment. Here again, the dual state functions as a structural prerequisite for genocide. The German railway transports ordinary Germans to a destination while the same railway system is used by the RuSHA to deport Jews to be killed.

As it evolved from pre-to wartime functions, the camp system also grew in scope and scale. In large part, the camps operated with a dual purpose, to function as a vast network for slave labor and to destroy the racial enemies of the Nazi regime. The appearance of the death camps during the Holocaust shares a common feature with other states committed to genocidal practices with an emphasis on speed and efficiency. All genocides are in essence shortlived bursts of extraordinary violence perpetrated by states determined to solve a perceived problem as quickly as possible. This is clearly the case with the death camps. Globocnick was assigned by Himmler the task of destroying the Jews of the General Government. To accomplish this task, Globocnick and his staff were made responsible for constructing and coordinating the deportation of the Jews, killing the Jews in the camps and the handling of the victims' valuables, in what became known as Operation Reinhard.

Chelmno was the first death camp to employ on a consistent and exclusive basis the use of gas vans. When the killing began there in December 1941, continuing until April 1943, the camp on an average day was capable of killing 1,000 victims from Poland, Germany, Austria, France, Belgium, Luxembourg and Holland. Chelmno was problematic for Nazi perpetrators due to chronic breakdowns in the destructive process. There were various complaints about problems associated with the use of the death vans, from the length of time necessary to kill, which often exceeded the standard fiften minutes, as well as mechanical problems and the killers' close proximity to victims. If anything, Chelmno provided the Nazis with examples of what to avoid. Consequently, the first of the three River Bug Death Camps, Belzec was constructed and operational as of March 1942 to exterminate the Jews of southeastern Poland. Instead of mobile gas vans, Belzec was a pioneer in the use of permanent gas chambers using carbon monoxide. At its peak, Belzec had a killing capacity of 15,000 per day and overall killed approximately 600,000 Jews. In Belzec, though, efforts to avoid a breakdown were not entirely successful. Breakdown did result from the killing method, which actually resulted in slowing, not accelerating, the pace of extermination. The "Hackenholt" method of frequent gassing resulted in delays, with many victims waiting for hours to die inside the gas chambers. With an average of forty to sixty freight cars arriving at Belzec each day and only room for twenty in the reception area, these slowdowns were a common occurrence. Adjustments were made, such as the addition of larger gas chambers and suspension of transports in the event of backlogs.

Sobibor was both a transitional and trendsetting death camp. It was transitional in the sense that it filled the killing gap, while Treblinka and Auschwitz were developing as far more sophisticated centers of mass murder. At the same time, the emphasis on avoiding breakdown in the killing process at Sobibor came to play a key role in the development of Treblinka and Auschwitz. This concern was expressed during the construction of Sobibor in April 1942, when Globocnick appointed Stangl commandant of Sobibor. Globocnick ordered Stangl to visit Belzec with Wirth in order to gain knowledge needed to improve the practice of mass murder in Sobibor. Stangl, another veteran of the Euthanasia program described his visit to Belzec:

> I went there by car. As one arrived, one reached Belzec railway station, on the left side of the road. . . The smell. . . oh God, the smell. It was everywhere. Wirth wasn't in his office. I remember they took me to see him. . . he was standing on a hill next to the pits. . . the pits. . . they were full.[12]

At Sobibor, various improvements were put in place that were designed to prevent breakdown, such as streamlined liquidation of the transports:

> . . .a narrow-gauge mine truck that ran from the railroad platform to the mass graves in Camp III. It was to replace the carts pulled by prisoners or horses, which had transported the dead, the sick and invalids from the train to the ditches.[13]

Another lesson of Belzec improved upon at Sobibor was the increase in the capacity of the gas chambers. At Belzec, breakdown occurred if the number of victims exceeded the gas chamber's capacity. At Sobibor, new gas chambers were constructed in September 1992: "The new gas chambers were able to accomodate four thousand people at a time, the old ones only six hundred."[14] Another improvement over Belzec designed to prevent a slowdown in the killing was the invention of a set procedure to deal with a set number of transports.

> The deportation trains stopped at the station of Sobibor. No more than eighteen to twenty freight cars were taken into the camp. When the train was comprised of more cars, it was split into two or three parts. The escort and railway workers

remained outside the camp, and only a specially trusted team of German railway workers drove the train inside.[15]

Another effort to prevent breakdown was the handling of transports that arrived at night: ". . .they disembarked and were kept under guard in Camp II until the morning. Then they were taken to undress and to the gas chambers. Usually no extermination activity was carried out in the dark."[16] Rapid processing of the victims was another important method used in all the death camps. From the transports to the gas chambers, the victims, with the exception of a brief interval, were kept constantly on the move.

As of July 1942, Treblinka stood ready to accomplish one goal, the killing of Jews from the Warsaw Ghetto, Germany, Austria, Czechoslovakia, Holland, Belgium and France. From July 1942 to the fall of 1943, the ultimate goal was to increase the number of victims. Treblinka came to represent a technical achievement of avoiding breakdown in the killing. The first Commandant of Treblinka, Eberl was relieved of his command because his management of Treblinka led to a breakdown in the killing.

Conditions at his camp were indescribable because he kept on sending new Jews to be killed before the bodies of those killed in earlier operations had been removed, i.e. disposed of. Thus the first sight the new Jewish arrivals saw as they got off the train at Treblinka was piles of corpses, partly in advanced stages of decomposition, so that they understood at once what was in store for them. [17]

Stangl, who learned much about making death a smooth operation at Sobibor, became the new commandant. When he was responsible for the overall running of Treblinka, it was Franz, the deputy camp commandant, who assumed an important role in preventing a slowdown in the killing process. Franz became very involved in the day to day operations of Treblinka and made important changes in the handling of the corpses and the supervision of incoming transports. An important concern for Franz and Stangl was how to liquidate the large number of transports arriving without a significant slowdown in killing. At one peak period, from August to December 1942, ". . .one to three transports would arrive at Treblinka each day. Each transport consisted of an average of 60 boxcars and each boxcar held between 80 and 150 people."[18] There was another obstacle that threatened to slow down the killing, the disposal of corpses. "Initially, the corpses were transported to the mass graves in small-gauge railway cars, These cars were moved by inmates running in double-time tempo. As a result, there were frequent breakdowns when the cars jumped the tracks."[19] At first, this emphasis on increasing the death rate and taking in larger and larger transports led to a breakdown in the destructive machinery:

Because the gassing facilities were prone to technical breakdowns, the camp was
unable to cope with such an enormous amount of people. Those who could not
be forced inside the gas chambers were shot in the reception camp. More and
more prisoners and more and more ditches were needed to bury all those who
had been shot.[20]

It was at this time that Stangl and Franz realized that in order to increase the death rate, more reforms were needed. One solution was to increase the size of the gas chambers. Initially, the camp's three small gas
chambers were too small to deal with the large number of ever-increasing
transports. What became a top priority for Stangl was to construct a new
building for gas chambers next to the other ones. Gassing expert Hock-
enholt who had experience running gas chambers in Belzec, was sent by
Wirth to Treblinka to assist in setting up the new gas chambers. The capacity of these new gas chambers was almost double the killing capacity of
the chambers in the old house, ". . .the new gas chambers could absorb a
maximum of 2,300 people (six chambers) or 3,800 people (ten chambers)
simultaneously, whereas the old one could hold only 600."[21]
Another reform that sped up the processing of victims was the way in
which corpses were disposed. As of spring 1943, the Nazis began to cremate the corpses instead of bury them. A large grill was constructed with
an enormous fire underneath, which was used to cremate the Jews in the
gas chambers. An elevator was used to dig up buried corpses, so they now
could be cremated. Most of all, breakdown was minimized by an elaborate division of labor that kept the assembly line of death moving. From
start to finish, every aspect of this production line was carefully timed.
Stangl described it as the processing of "cargo." Processing of the incoming victims was the responsibility of SS men, Germans and Ukranians and
a larger number of worker Jews, victims who were given a temporary stay
of execution. Eventually, a standard operating procedure was put in place
that began even prior to the arrival of the transports.

As the train approached the extermination center, the engine blew a prolonged
whistle, which was the signal for the Ukranians to man their positions in the reception center and on the roofs of the buildings. One group of SS men and Ukranians
took up positions on the station platform. As soon as the train was moving along
the tracks inside the camp, the gates behind it were closed. The deportees were tak-
en out of the freight cars and conducted through a gate to a fenced-in square inside
the camp. At the gate, they were separated: men to the right, women to the left.[22]

At this point, the elaborate deception began, the express purpose of
which was to speed the victims along, thereby preventing them from slowing down their own destruction. Men were led to one undressing barrack,

women and children to another for the so-called shower. Clothes were tied into neat bundles. Valuables were turned over. Naked women and children were forced into the "tube." Along the way, they were beaten and whipped. The procedure was the same for males except that they were gassed after the women and children. Within different parts of the camp, Jews were forced to participate in the destruction of other Jews. In the reception area, Platform workers, Transport square workers, "Gold Jews," Haircutters and a Sorting team were involved in the processing of the victims leading to their deaths. Within the killing area, there was a gas chamber, body disposal unit, tube cleaners, a body transport team, dentists and a burial detail. The sick and elderly who could not participate in the rapid march to death were sent to the Treblinka infirmary for a permanent "cure," a shot to the back of the neck. This assembly line of death could handle a transport in forty-five minutes. An entire transport consisting of twenty trains with twenty cars each, carrying a total of 24,000 Jews could be disposed of between 7 a.m. and 1:30 p.m.

What can be understood from an analysis of the operation and function of the death camps is how the dual state is reproduced. With the evolution of the death camps, what we have, in essence, is that the reproduction of the dual state is driven by an ever-expanding search to increase the scale and scope of mass killing. This ever-increasing amount of victims supports the dual state and maintains its sense of purpose. So the death camps represent the organization and implementation of bureaucratic killing whose existence is predicated on the manufacture of death, thus the dual state is reproduced. It also means that the reproduction of the dual state is crisis-driven, in the sense that without the creative destructiveness which drives the functioning of this state, the state will break down if the SS continually fails to reinvent and expand the mass killing. If the bureaucratic reproduction of the dual state is to continue, the novel mass murder techniques which were pioneered in the death camps must be further developed. This helps to explain the appearance of Auschwitz and its novel contribution to the mass murder of the Jews. More Jews died in Auschwitz than in any other camp or place during the Holocaust. Auschwitz became the embodiment of perfected mass killing with a continental reach during the Final Solution, killing Jews from all parts of Eastern and Western Europe. What is striking about Auschwitz is that its history provides further evidence of the "creative destructiveness" of the dual state.

At first, Auschwitz was not intended to become the epicenter of the Holocaust. For Auschwitz was geographically located in order to serve the specific political and economic goals of Lebensraum and to supply German industry with natural resources. The shifting mission of Auschwitz coincided with Nazi Germany's war aims and the shift in direction toward the Final Solution. This would all occur during the fateful second half of 1941 when Auschwitz would begin to assume a role in the Final Solution. At this time, Hoss, according to his testimony, spoke of his meeting with Himmler in the summer of 1941, in which he was told of Hitler's decision to exterminate the Jews. It was not long after Hoss met with Himmler that Eichmann arrived at Auschwitz. Eichmann's authority and control over the deportation process would grow when Auschwitz's role in the Final Solution was expanded.

In 1941 and for much of 1942, the death camps assumed the central role in the killing of Jews. By September 1941, we have the first indications that Auschwitz's role in mass killing was in the experimental stages. In September 1941, 850 prisoners were the victims of the experimental gassing using Prussic acid or Zyklon B. In December, another group of prisoners was gassed using Zyklon B in what was at the time the mortuary of the Auschwitz Crematorium. There were additional gassings of prisoners in two farmhouses in Birkenau in March and June of 1942. The scale of the gassings in Auschwitz were limited to those that took place in the crematorium of Auschwitz I and the two farmhouses in Birkenau until March 1943. Nonetheless, in summer 1942, four crematoria were being planned for Birkenau. This combination of gas chamber and oven would by June 1943 transform Auschwitz into a murder factory, which would with the adjustments made during the arrival of Hungarian Jews, make Auschwitz the camp that murdered more Jews than Treblinka. Daily estimates of the number of victims that could be killed in the crematorium are made, according to the industrial planners. "Crematorium I—340 corposes, Crematorium II—1440 corpses, Crematorium III—1440 corpses, Crematorium IV—768 corpses, Crematorium V—768 corpses."[23] On any given day, "all the crematoria together would therefore burn 4,756 corpses. . . "[24] Crematorium II and Crematorium III account for the largest number of Jewish victims during their operation. Crematorium II was in operation from March 31, 1943 to November 27, 1944, annihilating a total of 400,000 people. Crematorium IV functioned from June 25, 1943 to November 27, 1944, killing approximately 350,000 victims. In keeping with the industrial mindset that constructed these assembly lines of death, all aspects were carefully planned so that the process of mass murder followed set procedures. What was in the minds of the perpetrators was to design these facilities so that the victims were killed as quickly as possible and to put in place procedures which would prevent any slowdown of this destructive machinery. Deception was a key element used to keep this assembly line of killing moving at a rapid pace. In the case of crematoria II and III, there was barbed wire fencing, trees and bushes to hide the facilities and control the movement of those victims who entered to be processed. The underground undressing rooms were designed to deceive with hooks to hang up clothing along with instructions on the walls in various languages supplemented by the verbal commands given by the SS. Speed and deception were the hallmarks that characterized how the assembly line of death operated.

> In the Crematorium yard, the SS men told the prisoners that they would undergo a disinfection that consisted of delousing and bathing. The victims were led down the staircase to the dressing room in the basement, where they could see the signs (in German) 'To the baths' and 'To Disinfection.' Similar signs were posted on a portable board in the native language of the victims.[25]

The last part of this assembly line for the victims was the killing in the gas chamber.

> On the way to the gas chamber, some victims were issued a piece of soap and towel. As a rule, women and children went in first, followed by the men. Each group was led inside the chamber behind a cordon of SS men that edged toward the door as the chamber was filled. When the chamber was filled or the entire transport was inside. . .the doors were shut. . . on the order of the supervising SS doctor. . . the SS disinfectors opened the Zyklon B cans and poured their contents into the vents. . . Within several minutes, 20 at most, all the victims were dead.[26]

The factory style killing at Auschwitz provides evidence that the genocidal functioning of the dual state is reproduced by inventing new means with which to increase the ability to engage in mass killing. The creation of the crematoria in Birkenau achieves this goal. The majority of Jews killed at Auschwitz were in the crematoria of Birkenau.

Notes

1. Michael Burleigh, *The Third Reich* (New York: Macmillan Press, 2000) p. 122
2. *Ibid* p. 123
3. *Ibid* p. 124
4. *Ibid*
5. Heinz Hohne, *The Order of the Death's Head* (New York: Ballantine Books, 1989) p.

50

6. *Ibid* p. 164

7. Hans Frank, excerpt from Nuremberg Trials transcript, quoted from minutes of governmental conference, August 24, 1942 cited from http://www.yale.edu/lawweb/avalon/imt/proc/02-25-46.htm

8. Henry Friedlander, "Euthanasia and the Final Solution in David Cesarani" in *The Final Solution* (New York: Routledge Press, 1994) p. 56

9. Ernst Klee, Willie Dresser, Volker Riess, *Those Were the Days* (UK: Hamnish Hamilton, 1991) p. 61

10. *Ibid* p. 80

11. Uwe Adam, "The Gas Chambers" in *Unanswered Questions: Nazi Germany and the Genocide of the Jews* (New York: Schocken Books, 1989) p. 140

12. Gitta Sereny, *Into that Darkness* (New York: Vintage Press, 1983) p. 111

13. Eugen Kogon, *Nazi Mass Murder: A Documentary History of the Use of Poison Gas* (New Haven: Yale University Press, 1993) p. 133

14. *Ibid* p. 133

15. Yitzhak Arad, *Belzec, Sobibor, Treblinka* (Bloomington: Indiana Press, 1987) p. 75

16. *Ibid* p. 75

17. Alexander Donat, *The Death Camp Treblinka* (New York: Holocaust Library, 1979) p. 303

18. *Ibid* p. 52

19. *Ibid* p. 301

20. Kogon, p. 127

21. Arad, p. 120

22. Kogon, p. 125

23. Franciszek Piper, *Auschwitz 1940-1945 Vol. III* (Oswiecim: Auschwitz State Museum, 2000) p. 159

24. Piper, "Gas Chambers and Cremation" in *Anatomy of the Auschwitz Death Camp* (Indianapolis: Indiana University Press, 1994) p. 164

25. *Ibid* p. 169

26. Piper, p. 470

Chapter 5

The Structure of the State and Genocide in the Developing World

Given the enormous human cost, civilian and military, during World War II, especially the continent-wide dimensions of the Holocaust, humanity seemed to have reached a turning point in recognizing and beginning to halt genocidal practices, with the Nuremberg trials and the United Nations Genocide Convention. Not to downplay the importance of those events, but they failed to develop an effective global strategy to rein in state power, especially in the developing world where genocides proliferated after 1945. By and large, if there is a global mind set among nation-states, it is characterized by the idea that the sovereign authority of a nation is untouchable when it comes to a nation's deployment of its coercive might. There are no clear examples of genocides prevented or halted. Nation-states are free to act primarily against their own citizens, engaging in genocidal practices without intervention from other nation-states.

In developing countries, genocides have followed a similar pattern. The nature of how they develop can be traced back to the process of state formation, whereby a colonial legacy is followed by decolonialization. During this time of transition, as the nation is struggling to form an autonomous state, the pre-conditions for genocide appear. In this process of state formation, the colonial legacy creates a "weak state," weak in the sense that the state lacks democratic support, is ruled by an elite and holds onto power through force. For these newly formed states, the overriding concern is to control the populace within its territorial boundaries. In addition, a state which is overdetermined by military and police powers, is supervigilant as to identifying any opposition to its authority. When the state considers a threat serious enough, a crisis of the state's authority results and the state ideologically mobilizes against it. With this step, a "dual state" is created, the purpose of which is to use extraordinary violence to confront the threat. Once the victims are identified, the state will commit itself to genocidal measures, exerting its right to use a monopoly of force and violence. In order to illustrate this theory of genocide in the developing world, these countries will serve as illustrations: Indonesia (1965-1966); East Timor (1975); Cambodia (1975-1978) and Rwanda (1990-1994).

Indonesia

Indonesia's colonial legacy dates back to the 17th century with the Dutch East India Company. By the early 20th century, in response to economic exploitation, the Indonesian National Party was formed under the leadership of Sukarno. The struggle for independence from the Dutch was achieved when Indonesia was liberated in 1949, the result of a combination of world opinion and American pressure. Sukarno became President, motivated by the goal to modernize Indonesia with his support rooted in the Army.

Of the political parties founded during and after Indonesia's independence, the most influential one was the PKI, the Indonesian Communist Party, one of Indonesia's two power centers. The other was the military. Prior to and during independence, tensions rose between the two. During the final years of the struggle against the Dutch, the Communists had a strong presence within many Army units as well as influence among junior army officers. The commanders were concerned about a possible Communist takeover. Opposition to the Communists also came from the Orthodox Islam community, fearing that once in power, Communists would impose a secular state. The Communists were also opposed by the Indonesian National Party, which represented the interests of the technocratic-bureaucratic elites.

These concerns were heightened when Sukarno, recognizing the PKI's increasing electoral showing, incoporated Communist ideas into the state ideology in what he called "Guided Democracy." The party's interests and the state's interests appeared to merge, while at the same time, opposition to the PKI was increasing as it attempted to implement its policies. The "Gestapu Affairs" of September 30 and October 1, 1965 set the stage for genocidal messages. A faction within the PKI attempted a coup to transfer state control to a Revolutionary Council. Part of the plan involved the kidnapping and eventual murder of six members of the military high command. In less than twenty-four hours, the coup was halted by the military under the command of Major-General Suharto.

At this time, a dual state was formed by the Army's Supreme Operational Command to crush what it identified as the Gestapu, a term it used to convey the diabolical nature of the opposition as akin to the Nazi Gestapo. It was only days after the recovery of the bodies of the generals that the headquarters of the PKI was destroyed. The dual state was operating under the direction of an organization known as "The Operational Command for the Restoration of Security and Order" answering to Suharto. Its purpose was to locate, arrest and punish those known to have been involved in the Gestapu affair, also referred to as the September 30th movement. Ideological mobilization by the dual state was underway:

> Within days of the failures of the 30th September movement, the commanders of the Army's strategic reserve, Kostrad, and of the paracommando unit RP-KAD, together with their allies, embarked on a deliberate campaign to promote a climate of fear and retribution. A crucial element was a propaganda campaign, especially during October and November, aimed at creating popular fear and loathing of the PKI and its supporters. [1]

The intention was to whip up popular support and participation in the persecution and mass killing of the PKI and its supporters. The ideological mobilization amounted to an entire propaganda campaign against the perceived threat that the PKI posed to the state. This campaign united the state perpetrators and society in a joint effort to support the unleashing of state power to destroy the PKI. "The kill or be killed atmosphere was heightened soon after Gestapu by the appearance in virtually all regions where mass killings later occurred of alleged death lists, purported to have been drawn up by the PKI in preparation for a post-coup extermination of anti-Communists."[2] With the ideological mobilization by the Indonesian state, the military formed an alliance with those groups hostile to the PKI to perform coordinated actions, which lead to wholesale murder of the PKI and its sympathizers. "In the second half of October 1965, groups of anti-Communist youth in Central and East Java, mostly belonging to Islamic and Christian organizations, began mass killings of alleged PKI sympathizers."[3] While the state's ideological mobilization enlisted the populace to destroy the PKI, it also dispatched the military to kill PKI members and associates. "Under Army supervision, and with Army participation, large scale massacres took place in Central and East Java, Bali and Northern Sumatra."[4]

Overall, it was the development of a dual state that was instrumental in developing and implementing genocidal practices. For through the creation of the Operational Command for the Restoration of Security and Order or Kopkamtib, "Between December 1965 and March 1966 the state's management of violence shifted from military promoted killings at the local level to much more centrally-directed arrests and detention of Old Order remnants, carried out through the Kopkamtib apparatus."[5] What was happening at that time was the dual state was disseminating an ideology to support the violent measures against the PKI. This is the underlying intention behind the signing of the decree of March 1966 ". . .President Sukarno was compelled to sign the now famous instruction of 11 March or Supersenar, empowering Suharto, newly appointed as Minister/Army commander to: Take all monies considered necessary to ensure peace and order and stability of the revolution . . .in the intents of the nation and state of the Republic of Indonesia."[6] What this means is that mass killing is now under the control of the dual state controlled by Suharto and the military. With genocidal practices, the dual state can act independent of the legitimate state without any legal limits. In the case of Indonesia, as a result of competition for control in the post-colonial period, the state's inability to deal with internal threats to state power lead to an effort to compensate for this weakness, by expanding state power. Through the seizure of power by the military, state power was intensified. In so doing, a dual state was created with the military in charge. As a result, the state would exercise without any legal limit a right to employ a monopoly of force and violence. This result is apparent if consideration is given to the effects of the massacres: "First, was the elimination of the leadership of the PKI and the destruction of its mass cadre structure. Second, it issued an unequivocal warning to those who might consider a challenge to the new ruling elite."[7] With the genocidal massacres, the dual state served to legitimate this form of state power and the state's right to destroy its enemies. Mass killing is the purpose of the dual state: ". . .The measures were promoted by the state and implemented by a combination of state direction and communal fervor. Thus, the scale of mass murder meted out against PKI members and supporters endorsed the party and its allies as 'traitors,' also making them responsible for the violence itself. Finally, the violence in turn endorsed the dependence of the state upon the military for the maintenance of internal order and enabled the consolidation of military-bureaucratic state power."[8]

In the case of the genocidal measures waged against the PKI, the dual state in Indonesia would use mass killing and the ideology in support of it to unite Indonesia. The genocidal massacre of the PKI by the dual state served to settle the question of state use of violence, its right to employ it and control civil society. Ultimately, in Indonesia, an autonomous state was tantamount to a state able and willing to wage war against its own citizens, thus claiming a legitimate right to exercise a monopoly over violence. When perpetrators are convinced that the threat posed by an identified victim group is immediate and direct, the violent coercive arm of the state sets out to destroy it. What drives this concerted effort by the state to destroy is a chain of events leading to a state crisis. The state is compelled by a sense of urgency that the threat is so pervasive and immediate that the victims must be dealt with right away.

East Timor

But what if the state identifies a long-term threat to its power? This question takes us to the example of East Timor. As events unfolded in East Timor during the 1970s, we have the Indonesian state confronting an indirect threat to its authority. Two elements are pivotal to understanding this confrontation, East Timor's longstanding history as a colonial possession and Indonesia's aggressive colonialism, at the same time, ". . .vigorously asserting its own claim for the 'return of West Irian.'"[9]

East Timor was a colony of Portugal for over four centuries. Indonesia showed little interest in East Timor until a movement for independence led by two political parties, the Fretilin and UPT. For an Indonesia fixated on confronting any Communist or leftist organizations, the Fretilin was a convenient target. Also, Indonesia's concern over the drive for independence was based on a fear that it could spread elsewhere. For Indonesia, the solution was to integrate East Timor, placing it under control of the Indonesian military. This solution became all the more obvious as Portugal was in the process of withdrawing from East Timor. At this point, an Indonesian general was implementing "Operasi Komodo," a code named for an action to undermine the independence movement, especially the Fretilin. Having failed to halt the Fretilin, the pressure was now on to send troops in. For the leaders in the Fretilin, this was an opportunity to declare East Timor independent. For Indonesia, that was the justification to invade. Indonesian troops ". . . engaged in an orgy of indiscriminate killing, rape and torture. Large-scale public executions were carried out, women being included among the victims, suggesting a systematic campaign of terror. In some villages, whole communities were slaughtered, except for young children."[10] Nonetheless, the Indonesian troops faced stiff resistance by a compact Timorese Army. To the surprise of the Indonesian military, the hit-and-run style guerrilla operations of the Timorese Army were inflicting high casualties on the invaders. In response to this determined resistance, the Indonesian troops started targeting civilians.

> In Dili, there were a number of public executions, including at the Wharf area where more than 100 were reportedly shot at Santa Cruz, at the military police barracks and at Tasitolo, near the airport. Also, in the small towns of Maubara and Liquica and at other villages in the interior, Indonesian military units carried out public executions, numbering from 20 to 100 persons.[11]

What appeared to be unfolding was a consistent pattern of massacres which, by and large, targeted civilians. Still, while civilians are being murdered, there was no clear policy to kill all the Timorese people. The Indonesian Army was forced to adjust to fight a guerrilla war as the Timorese fighters and populace sought refuge and a base of operations in the mountainous interior. Forced to flee the mountainous interior, many Timorese were dying from famine and disease. What was becoming apparent to the

Indonesian state was that its use of force to overcome a threat was turning into a drawn-out struggle to subdue an elusive adversary. The Indonesian state was realizing, as so many would-be perpetrators do, that intense and rapid killing is not possible, so, as with most, they learn to invent, shifting gears to engage in the long-term destruction of the Timorese. This policy starts with the isolation of East Timor from external aid: ". . .East Timor was virtually sealed off from the outside world. The International Red Cross, which had been present in strength until just before the invasion, did not regain access to the territory until the second half of 1979, almost four years after the invasion."[12]

The physical isolation of the Timorese people also contributed to the destruction of their culture. The Indonesian government was undermining the essence of Timorese culture, to exist as a people independent from foreign rule. In other words, while genocide physically destroys a people, ethnocide destroys those aspects which shape and ultimately define a people's culture. During the conquest of East Timor, this ethnocide was state policy, ". . .destroying a distinguishing characteristic of the Timorese personality, in effect, changing their identity from that of a people seeking to shape their own political destiny to that of a compliant component of the Indonesian state."[13] The case study of Indonesian policy toward East Timor reveals how ethnocide becomes a useful option in confronting an indirect threat to state power.

Cambodia

In the case of Cambodia, the genocidal practices that unfolded during the reign of the Khmer Rouge can be traced to the post-colonial legacy of a country striving to construct a strong state capable of exercising territorial control. Post-colonial Cambodia was a nation confronted by internal and external threats. If there is a pattern of rule from Sihanouk and Lon Nol to Pol Pot it is of rulers who were attempting to exercise what they believed to be the legitimate right of the state to employ force in pursuit of state objectives. In support of this goal, they used ideology to justify the state's actions.

In part, the chain of events leading to the genocidal practices of the Khmer Rouge begins with the idea that rapid and violent social change should be the essence of state policy. This idea was characteristic in the minds of those Cambodian student radicals who returned from Paris in the 1960s. Two ideological elements made up the core beliefs of the students, some of whom would become the leaders of the Khmer Rouge. Those elements were Stalinism and nationalism, the core of which was the idealized past greatness of Cambodia and its restoration. Another element was a deep-seated hatred of Vietnam as Cambodia's historical enemy and a key target of the Khmer Rouge during the genocide. Sihanouk's contradictory policies of suppression of Communists within Cambodia, while supporting them in Vietnam only served to foster opposition to his regime. In addition, the wholesale corruption, so much a functioning part of the Sihanouk regime, served to further illustrate a government that was out of touch with the needs of its peasant majority.

The demise and eventual overthrow of the Sihanouk regime was, in large part, the result of a state undermined by a combination of internal and external factors. Its chief external threat was the destabilization of the regime caused by the United States' extension of the Vietnam War into Cambodia, culminating with the bombing campaign. With a weakened Cambodian state whose territorial control was diminished by external threat, the political climate was ripe for a coup d'etat by General Lon Nol, while also setting the stage for the rise of Pol Pot and the Khmer Rouge. Both Lon Nol and the Khmer Rouge intended to strengthen the coercive might and territorial control of the Cambodian state. Once in power, the Khmer Rouge would create a state in which the radical and forceful reorganization of territory led to genocide. A utopian ideology would serve to both justify and mobilize support for genocidal practices. The territorial controls would work in tandem with a state policy, which initiated a form of social engineering. Evidence for this interpretation appears in a meeting held on May 20, 1975. At this meeting, Pol Pot spoke of eight key provisions:

1. Evacuate people from all towns.
2. Abolish all markets.
3. Abolish Lon Nol regime currency and withhold the revolutionary currency that had been printed.
4. Defrock all Buddhist monks and put them to work growing rice.
5. Execute all leaders of the Lon Nol regime beginning with the top leaders.
6. Establish high-level cooperatives throughout the country, with communal eating.
7. Expel the entire Vietnamese minority population.
8. Dispatch troops to the borders, particularly the Vietnamese border.[14]

As part of its territorial organization, the Khmer Rouge in April 1975 divided the country with several zones: the southwest, the northeast, the north, the northwest and a special zone near the capital city of Phnom Penh. Forceful territorial reorganization was exemplified by the mass evacuation of Phnom Penh. The Khmer Rouge justified this evacuation based on a fear of enemies in cities which the Khmer Rouge viewed as centers of groups opposed to the regime. This was the first step in which a Khmer Rouge state made an effort to enforce a claim to the right to use violence in service of territorial control. The genocidal practices, which unfolded as a result of the evacuation, combined the state's use of extraordinary violence to control and reshape Cambodian territory, supported by utopian ideology. The mass evacuation of Phnom Penh reveals ideological contradiction in the state's utopian justification for this action. On the one hand, the state's drive to collectivize is forward-looking, while on the other, its utopian ideology looks to the past, in order to ". . . recover its pre-Buddhist glory by rebuilding the powerful economy of the medieval Angkor Kingdom and regain lost territory from Vietnam and Thailand."[15]

Using the rationalization that political enemies were based in cities, such as Phnom Penh, the Khmer Rouge had begun taking incremental steps toward mass killing by identifying so-called enemies, the group called the "New People." These were a mixture of officials, both military and administrative, from Lon Nol's regime, religious leaders, intellectual and cultural figures, bureaucrats and technocrats. They were the first victims of the Khmer Rouge on orders given by the newly formed state structure of Democratic Kampuchea, the ruling body known as the Standing Committee of the Communist Party of Kampuchea, the leadership of which bore responsibility for the unfolding genocide. Known as the party center or high organization, it represented a specialized state apparatus whose purpose was to make the political decisions that then would be implemented, ultimately destroying Cambodian society. The Khmer Rouge created a state without legal limits, free to act without restraint, whose sole authority is derived from its ability to unleash extreme violence. The political aims of this state in terms of territorial reorganization would merge with its genocidal measures. The reorganization allowed the Khmer Rouge to eventually centralize control.

> One aim of the CPK center was to build larger and larger units at the local level, abolishing village life altogether in favor of 'high-level cooperatives,' the size of a subdistrict. At the other end of the hierarchy, the center set about reducing the autonomy of the zones by bringing them under its own control. [16]

Given this background, the initial genocidal measures taken against the "New People" were carried out by a state seeking to gain coercive control over territory and eliminate perceived threats. With the mass evacuations under the Khmer Rouge under way, the harshest treatment was reserved for the New People who would perish in large numbers.

> These 'new' people were not granted even the few privileges of the 'old' people, the original peasants who were at first allowed no private property and had to work extremely hard, ten hours a day and often added hours at night, with limited food rations. Many of them starved. There was not enough food in the forest for

sustenance but the new people were forbidden to supplement their meager diets by foraging. Disease was rampant; medical care poor.[17]

It is no coincidence that the ethnic groups targeted by the Khmer Rouge and killed in large numbers were considered to be internal and external threats to its goal of coercive control over territory. For example, consider the fate of the Vietnamese: "Over 100,000. . . were driven out by the Pol Pot regime in the first year after its victory in 1971." [18] Consider the fact that some of the most intense killing was in the eastern zone, an area near the border between Cambodia and Vietnam. The ones who remained in Cambodia were simply murdered. As for the fate of the Chinese, "Of the 1975 population of 425,000, only 200,000 Chinese survived the next four years."[19]

The Khmer Rouge's utopian ideology of collectivization served to accelerate the mass killings. In Cambodia, the Khmer Rouge created a specialized or dual state, which seeks to control and transform Cambodia by violent means. What is unique about this transition to a dual state is the decline in the capacity of the non-genocidal part of the Cambodian state, which reproduces the foundation of social existence. Mass murder becomes the dominant function of the state, while there is, at the same time, a unique degeneration of legitimate state functions. Under the Khmer Rouge, the non-genocidal part of the Cambodian state breaks down. The Khmer Rouge's dismantling of the family illustrates a fundamental disregard for an institution necessary for social reproduction.

> Normal family life, including love and sorrow, was impossible in some villages. Children were taken away from their parents to live and work in brigades. If they died of fatigue or disease, which many did, their parents would eventually be informed. At this point, what emotion the parents showed could mean life or death. If they wept or displayed extreme unhappiness, this showed bourgeois sentimentality.[20]

Other aspects important to the continuity of Cambodian society, such as the culture of peasant life, were under attack by the Khmer Rouge, in particular, Buddhism, which was

> . . . a state religion and the priesthood of monks with their saffron robes a central part of Cambodian culture. Some 90 percent of Cambodians believed in some form of Buddhism and many had received a rudimentary education from the monks. Indeed, it was customary for young people to become monks for part of their lives. So central and locally powerful an institution could not be allowed to be independent so the Khmer Rouge set out with vigor to destroy it. Monks were defrocked; many were simply executed.[21]

Another indication that non-genocidal functions had broken down appears in the mass evacuation of the cities, which served as the cultural and intellectual centers. Collectivization was destroying Cambodian society. The self-destructive elements of collectivization indicate a state guided by extreme violence, working against its own utopian ideology. All too often, the agricultural production quotas were not met and resistance to collectivization was increasing.

Rwanda

The genocide that took place in Rwanda in 1994, was in large part the product of state formation during colonialism and post-colonialism. During both periods, the Rwandan state functioned to maintain social divisions. These unresolved social divisions would ultimately be resolved by the use of extreme violence. With the identification of the group in question as the source of both internal and external threats, a specialized part of the state assumed the role of organizing and mobilizing support to destroy it. The divide and conquer mentality of the colonizers allowed the Belgians to construct a system of indirect rule by manufacturing differences between the Tutsi and Hutu. By elevating what was Tutsi and degrading what was Hutu, the Belgians could enlist the support of the Tutsi in administering Rwanda. This elevation of the Tutsi was nothing more than the creation of racial myths. The Tutsi were defined as a group that had its origins elsewhere. Rwandan culture was identified as the product of the Tutsis, who were depicted as "the hidden hand behind every bit of civilization on the continent. . . "[22] The Tutsi were identified as an alien race, not native to Rwanda. The Tutsi were also defined as a privileged minority in sharp contrast to the native majority, the Hutus. Given this division, the Tutsi, defined as the bearers of civilization, would come to occupy a privileged position in various institutions, in particular, schools and local administration. On the other hand, the Hutu were denied a voice and excluded from having any semblance of power in Rwandan institutions. Even though a small number of Tutsi elites held privileged positions in state and social institutions, the perception among the Hutus was to regard the Tutsi as aligned with the colonizers, embodying an air of superiority.

The racial divide between Tutsi and Hutu was given legal standing when the colonial state used a census to further define the Tutsi and the Hutu. The 1933-1934 census defined the races in terms of ownership of property, especially cattle. In order to be counted as Tutsi, a citizen had to own at least ten head of cattle, "the ten cow rule." The colonial church was the institution that produced the raw data, which clearly were prejudiced in favor of the Tutsi. So the result is a colonial church working together with the colonial state to legitimize a racial divide. In effect, the Belgian colonial state defined the Tutsi and Hutu as two different races. This division allowed Belgium to maintain rule by defining the majority Hutu as the inferior indigenous majority and the Tutsi as a superior, non-indigenous minority. Given the colonial state's definition of these racial divisions, the only hope for a reversal would be decolonization. But instead, decolonization put Rwanda on the path to genocide, with the post-colonial state in many ways, maintaining these social divisions.

Decolonization was accomplished through a political and not a social revolution in the sense that power would change hands in the state but the underlying social basis of the conflict between the Tutsi and Hutu remained. The Revolution of 1959 was an uprising by a privileged Hutu elite, the product of the Belgian colonizers overturning traditional social relations. The Hutus believed that the goal behind the 1959 Revolution was to overturn Tutsi political domination, especially at the local level. The political essence of the 1959 revolution appears in a manifesto, "Notes on the Social Aspect of the Racial Native Problem in Rwanda" or the "Bahutu Manifesto." This manifesto clearly illustrates the social divisions, which are at the core of the conflicts between the Tutsi and Hutu. The 1959 revolution is also significant in that it was the embodiment of a struggle for political power between the Tutsi and the Hutu in terms of capturing state power. From this period up to the 1994 genocide, the state was the arbiter for settling these divisions and eventually state power would be used to violently settle this problem. From 1959-1994, the Rwandan state framed the conflict of Tutsi v. Hutu in territorial terms.

The state has at its disposal the use of force to organize social relations and maintain order within territorial boundaries. From 1959 to 1994, there was an acceleration of Rwanda's profound social crisis expressed in territorial terms. Overall, the Rwandan state's inability to effectively mediate this social crisis becomes a leading cause of genocide in Rwanda. The struggle between the Tutsi and the Hutu results in the creation in 1959 of various Tutsi and Hutu political parties, which are divided over who should rule. The Tutsi position amounted to an argument in support of preservation of its precolonial prerogatives. For the Hutu, independence meant majority rule. The Tutsi's were conscious of their power and they feared losing it; the Hutu view was of a group aware of its powerlessness. The Tutsi viewpoint, in the long run, could only be self-defeating for the Tutsi wanted power in the name of tradition at the expense of an indigenous majority. Given such polarized positions, it is not surprising that such a struggle for political control would lead to violence. The social crisis was displaced to the state level with the state alternating between mediation and violence.

An example of this tendency appears in what became known as the Mwana coup, wherein Tutsi's replaced the deceased Mwani (king) with an unqualified half-brother. The Hutu responded to this coup, which they viewed as anti-democratic, ever more determined to acquire state control, with the formation of Parmehutu, to win the upcoming elections. An early indication that violence would settle Tutsi-Hutu conflicts was an incident in late fall 1959. An attack on Dominique Mbonyumutwa, a Parmehutu leader, by a group of Tutsi UNAR members was the spark that led to an outbreak aghainst Tutsi chiefs and UNAR followers, resulting in 200 deaths. The violence accelerated in scale and level of violence, ". . . fighting followed, mostly with traditional weapons, such as spears, clubs and pangas. Many Tutsi houses were burnt, without making any distinction between high-lineage Tutsi and ordinary 'petit Tutsi.'" [23]

This violent outbreak had a ripple effect in terms of the Hutu becoming from this point an ever-increasing political and military presence during the period of transition to independence. Concerned over the violence, Belgium declared a state of emergency fearing not only a full-scale Hutu revolt, but also a Tutsi reaction. With the unrest showing no signs of dominishing, the Hutu were on their way to a takeover of local authority. The Belgian colonists came to the realization that since the presence of Tutsi chiefs was the source of the unrest, these chiefs must be replaced with Hutu chiefs: "More than three-hundred Hutu chiefs and subchiefs had replaced Tutsi incumbents who had been deposed, killed or had fled. . ." [24] Of greater significance was the decision by the Belgian authorities to support the Hutu administration with a Hutu military arm. This had the effect of swaying the outcome of many local elections in favor of the Hutu. It also served to inspire those supporters advocating Hutu control of the state. These steps lead to a mass movement seeking the end of the monarchy and the creation of a democratic republic. A provisional government was formed, followed by the election of a president of this new republic, Gregoire Kayibanda.

In response to the rise of Hutu power, the Tutsi elite had two responses, one segment went into exile while others stayed in Rwanda. Those who remained faced the prospect of adjusting and seeking a new place within Hutu society. For the exiles, the logical choice was nearby Burundi, which would in a short period of time become the launching pad for military attacks by the Tutsi exile community. At this point, the Rwandan state will begin to confront a possible threat to its territorial control by another nation. Faced with such a prospect, states over time have responded through the use of coercive might to defend national borders. This crisis fuels the internal perception that the Tutsis are an exceptional threat. The Tutsi exile community had one thing in mind, to undo the 1959 revolution and return to power. As early as 1962, those Tutsi seeking to restore their lost power began border attacks and ". . . undertook as many as ten known raids into Rwanda." [25] These attacks grew in scale and scope, especially with the Bugessera invasion of December 1963 which ". . . reached nearly twenty miles outside of Kigali."[26] The Rwandan state responded with reprisals. One such reprisal was in response to a border raid in 1962. The coercive arm of the Rwandan state after the border raid led to "Between 1000 and 2000 Tutsi men, women and children massacred and buried on the spot, their huts burned and pillaged and their property divided among the Hutu population."[27] While this was not the wholesale mass killing of 1994, it nonetheless is indicative of a state willing to use violence against a targeted group in support of its objectives.

These border attacks had another, disturbing long-term effect, to strengthen the Rwandan state as represented by President Kayibanda, the personification of Hutu rule. Another outcome of the killing of Tutsis in Rwanda was to dampen the interest of Tutsis living there in adapting to the new state of affairs while strengthening radical elements of the exiled Tutsi community who wanted to return to the past. Of still greater significance is the fact that the exile attacks served to strengthen those Hutus who supported the idea of Hutu power.

Well-aware of the ever-increasing conflict between Tutsi and Hutu, President Kayibanda attempted a moderate course in some ways. At the same time, he spoke as the leader of a Hutu nation, representing the political power of the Hutu, a role that was made clear by his actions to remove the Tutsi from political power.

> . . .Tutsi presence was forcibly removed from the political arena; the Tutsi were found in education, in business, in the church, even in government employment, but not in the political arena. The political sphere was confined to the Hutu, members of the Hutu nation.[28]

The measures taken during the Kayibanda regime link the colonial and post-colonial definitions of the Tutsi as an alien race, with the difference in the postcolonial era that the Tutsi are now deprived of political power.

The situation of the Tutsi is further complicated by what is viewed as the ever-growing external threat of an armed Tutsi exile community. The long-term effects are many. One effect stands out, and contributes to the genocide of 1994, the consequences of an armed Tutsi population that comes to power. The striking example for the Hutu is Burundi in 1972, in which a Tutsi minority, in an effort to maintain political control, carried out a massacre of the Hutu. No doubt this event impacted on events inside Rwanda and the local response, the creation of local defense groups, became the key aspect of the genocide in 1994. In the early 1970s, these groups did not have mass killing in mind. What is known is that these groups were then focused on what can be identified as the removal and concentration of Tutsi's, triggering another wave of Tutsi departures from Rwanda.

These vigilante groups not only removed the Tutsi from their jobs, they were responsible for spreading hate and fear of the Tutsi. While the Tutsi lacked political power, they had social power in terms of their representation in desired occupations, such as education and overall employment. Kayibanda faced growing criticism of what many Hutu regarded as his lack of attention to social inequality. Growing disenchantment with the slow pace of reform efforts by the Kayibanda regime and Hutu outcries about rich Tutsi and poor Hutu set the stage for a non-violent coup by Major-General Habyarimana.

At the start of this regime, we have the Tutsi's as a minority with social privileges but no political power. Throughout the Habyarimana reign, the Tutsi were excluded from political participation. "Throughout the Habyarimana years, there would not be a single Tutsi bourgmestre or perfect, there was one Tutsi officer in the whole army, there were two Tutsi members of parliament out of seventy and there was only one Tutsi minister out of a cabinet of between twenty-five and thirty members."[29] Due to the minority status of the Tutsi, as well as the ever-increasing ideology of Hutu power, another significant development was the reorganization of political control, in which power at the local level was dramatically increased. This was an important political reform of the Habyarimana regime. Overall, this does not mean Rwanda was in the purest meaning of the word, a democratic nation. There was little room for dissenting voices from the past and present. "Former President Kayibanda had died in detention in 1976, most likely starved to death by his gaolers."[30] Other former state officials of the Kayibanda regime were also killed. "Between 1974 and 1977, the security chief, Theoneste Lizinde, and his thugs, had killed fifty-six people, mostly former dignitaries of the Kayibanda regime."[31]

Nonetheless, economic downturns and a changing global climate more receptive to human rights in the 1980s put pressure on the Habyarimana regime to increase democratic participation in the form of creating a multi-party system. The invasion of the Tutsi-led RPF invasion would both quicken the pace of political reform and lead Rwanda closer to genocidal practices. What was taking place at this time was a structural transformation of the Rwandan state, drawing it into a greater partnership with civil society and creating an ideological alliance as well. The unfolding political and social crises of the early 1990s would only serve to further cement these ties in favor of the Hutu and against the Tutsi and eventually lead to genocide. How ironic it was that at the time of the RPF invasion of October 1990, the Habyaramina regime seemed to be making an effort to promote democratic participation in the form of a multi-party system. This invasion was the key event that would radicalize the Rwandan state and society to eventually use extraordinary violence against this combined external and internal threat. Underlying the chain of events which lead to genocidal practices waged against the Tutsi was a Rwandan state determined to claim and maintain its right to use extreme violence in order to control territory.

In part, the motive for the RPF invasion is easy to understand. With President Habyarimana accepting a multi-party system, the RPF was deprived of one of its main justifications to wage an armed struggle, that it was engaged in a fight against a one-party dictatorship. At this point in time, the formation of a dual state is taking place. Keep in mind that the key aspect of the dual state is that it is that specialized part of the state devoted to violently confronting and destroying the victim group, which is perceived as a threat. The formation of the Rwandan dual state was incremental. The state engages in piecemeal violent attacks against the Tutsi. Characteristic of this phase are the mass arrests, indiscriminate shooting and concentration of the Tutsi in holding centers and prisons. The emphasis inside Rwanda is clear, to take action against Tutsi civilians.

Between October 11 and October 13, an estimated 348 Tutsi civilians were massacred and more than 500 houses burned in the Kiliblira commune. None of the victims was a RPF fighter or a civilian supporter of whom there seemed to be none.[32]

Also emerging is another key element of the genocide, the links and coordination between the state and civil society. While the Rwandan state would begin to take the lead, creating a mobilizing ideology, the actual implementation and killing of the Tutsi was at the local level. This is the case with these initial killings, which, "in almost every case. . . were organized and led by local authorities."[33] A working partnership was developing between the emerging dual state and the peasants in Rwandan society. With this partnership, came a socialization process in which state and society were acquiring the means and most of all, the methods of engaging in violence and mass killing.

A common feature of all the measures is that they were preceded by political meetings during which a 'sensibilisation' process was carried out. These seemed to have been designed to put the people 'in the mood,' to drum into them that the people they were to kill were *ibyitso,* i.e. actual or potential collaborators of the RPF arch enemy. These meetings were always presided over and attended by the local authorities with whom the local peasants were familiar; but they usually featured the presence of an 'important person,' who would come from Kigali to lend the event an aura of added respectability and official sanction. After the 'sensibilisation' process had been carried out, the order would come sooner or later, either directly or indirectly from the Minister of the Interior in Kigali or the prefect.[34]

Through incremental episodic killings, the Hutu peasants were trained to accept killing Tutsi as acceptable. There were a series of these episodic killings ". . .the Mutara massacres of October 1990, the sporadic killings of the Bagogwe between the beginning of 1991 and early 1993, and the Munamti killings of November 1991."[35]

President Habyarimana, faced with a well-organized opposition, sought to promote order through mass arrests. It had the opposite effect of increasing resistance. What also comes to mind is a comparison to the Young Turks, who in the years prior to the genocide of the Armenians, believed in democratic reforms. So it was in Rwanda, with the democratic opposition, which wanted to prevent the Habyarimana regime from making the emergency measures permanent. At first, the ever-increasing conflict seemed to have been averted by President Habyarimana in his speech to the United National General Assembly, in which he proposed to address two of the demands of the RPF and the refugee community by granting "citizenship and travel documents to those who did not desire naturalization in their countries of asylum, and it could repatriate many of those who wished to return."[36] In addition to allowing for the existence of multiparties, Habyarimana permitted the formation of a coalition government, consisting of representatives from these parties.

It was also at this time that a small, extremist Hutu party appears, the Coalition for the Defense of the Republic or CDR, promoting the idea of the regime as too soft on the RPF and the Tutsi's. As sporadic killings took place, the Hutu peasants were indoctrinated with a mobilizing ideology, which would become essential in motivating Hutu peasants to kill the Tutsi's. The ideology promoted the view that "the RPF fighters were pictured as creatures from another world, with tails, horns, hooves, pointed ears and red eyes that shone in the dark."[37] These depictions became more widespread with RPF advances, at one point reaching to thirty kilometers of the capital Kigali. At this time, there were hundreds of thousands of Hutus fleeing the advancing RPF forces.

The Rwandan state was faced with a direct threat to its authority over its territorial boundaries. The possibility of diffusing the situation stemmed from the Arusha accords prompted by French intervention in this conflict. The political climate was influenced by an external Tutsi threat and the idea of Rwanda as a Hutu nation, thus, the accords were doomed to fail for there could be no compromises as far as the Hutu extremists were concerned. The exclusion of the Hutu from the Arusha peace process only served to fuel the idea that Habyarimana was biased in favor of the Tutsi. For the Hutu extremists, the evidence is clear, the accords favor the RPF, in that the RPF is power-sharing. Take the proposal for the RPF representation in the military, ". . .the RPF would provide 40 per cent of the soldiers in the new, national army but 50 per cent of the officer corps."[38]

Of greater significance is the concern by extremists that the Tutsi would have more political control over the physical might of the Rwandan state. ". . .the RPF was given charge of the important Ministry of the Interior. Together, these provisions gave the RPF decisive control over the forces of coercion in the new state. . ."[39]

Most of all, the extremist party, the CDR, would be denied any representation in the Parliament, a move that doomed the agreement and triggered actions designed to raise public opposition. This street opposition to the RPF as tied to the Tutsi in Rwanda, constituted internal and external threats, developed within the opposition parties, especially in their youth wing. These youth groups were nothing more than militia groups in particular, the Interahamwe (Those who Work and Fight Together), which became the fighting arm of the CDR. Here, again, is an essential precondition for genocide in Rwanda, a political organization with an ideological killing component. In a short period, they were to become the embodiment of the dual state in Rwanda. In one way, the Habyarimana regime had provided the groundwork for the Hutu extremists to form a dual state and a society in partnership with this state. The Habyarimana regime "in 1991 began a program to arm civilians and create 'self-defense' forces."[40] When the extremists assume control of the government, these self-defense units ". . . formed the civilian core of the machinery that came to carry out the genocide."[41] But, it was the dual state that issued the directives and instilled the idea that Hutu power and the preservation of it meant the elimination of the Tutsi threat.

The Habyarimana state set the stage for the genocide by the simple fact that it was a state bent on maintaining control by the use of force within and outside its borders. Mass killing was to emerge as the solution in which the ideological enemy, the Tutsi, once eliminated, would restore the power of the state. An important external spark, serving to ignite a state-society project to commit to the mass killing of the Tutsi, were events in Burundi. What took place in Burundi points to the Rwandan state's decision to use state power against a threat to its territory. Burundi had a Hutu president and government, but most important, it had an all-Tutsi Army. In a mere two months, during the Arusha accords, in October 1993, segments of the Tutsi Army murdered the president of Burundi. Given the Burundi example, there can be no doubt that for the Hutu extremists in Rwanda, the Tutsi posed real internal and external threats. The mass exodus of more than 200,000 Hutu entering Rwanda, makes clear to Hutu extremists the consequences of Tutsi power. The idea of power-sharing, which was the core of the Arusha accords, is impossible, given the situation in Burundi.

To Hutu extremists, there could only be one response, the formation of a dual state in Rwanda, which has a specialized ideological mission backed by a fighting force to confront the enemies of the state, the Tutsi minority. Given this chain of events, it is no coincidence that what we have is the Interahamwe and the Impuzamugambi as that part of the Rwandan state who believe the only way to preserve the Hutu's political power and defend the state is to destroy the Tutsi.

The only remaining obstacle to the formation of a genocidal state, restructured so as to organize and coordinate mass killing, was the removal of President Habyarimana, whose plane was shot down. The fact that wholesale killing began almost immediately after his death provides anecdotal evidence of a plot to kill him. "The plane was shot down at around 8:30 p.m., and by 9:15 there were already Interahamwe roadblocks everywhere in town and houses were being searched."[42] The killing squads of Interahamwe and Impuzamuganbi were about to commit themselves to a society-wide enterprise of killing Tutsi and Hutu sympathizers. "The death-lists had to be carefully distributed to the future killers, who acted in coordinated and systematic ways in order to catch their intended victims."[43] At this time, the house to house roundups and mass killings were underway. What is noteworthy is the elimination of those officials associated with the pre-genocidal state, the Prime Minister, Agatha Uniwdingiyimana, the head of the Constitutional Court, Joseph Kavarvganda, as well as the Minister of Agriculture Frederic Nzamurambaho and Foreign Minister Boniface Ngulinzira. Replacing them was a state whose primary purpose was to organize mass killing. Responsible for the government's role were the following perpetrators: ". . .Colonel Theoneste Bagosora, director of Services in the Ministry of Defence. . . Next in line is the Defense Minister, Major-General Augustin Bizimar. His military aides were mostly Colonel Aloys Ntabakuze. . . Lieutenant Colonel Protais. . . Lieutenant Leonard Nkundieye. . . Captain Pascal Simbikangua. . . "[44] Key military personnel were assisted by civilians within the state apparatus.

> . . . Joseph Nziorera, the Secretary General of MRND (D), who coordinated the Interahamwe operators; Pascal Musabe, a bank director, who was one of the militia organizers at the national level; the businessmen Felicien Kabuga, who financed the RTLMC and the Impuzamuganbi. . . . In the interior, the local organizers of the massacres were the prefects. . .[45]

Once this genocidal state was formed, it became a matter of coordination between the state and local killers within Rwandan society: ". . . the killers were controlled and directed in their task by the civil servants in the central government, prefects, bourgmestres and local councillors, both in the capital and the interior."[46] The actual killing was a local affair with the militias recruited from those who were unemployed, with criminal records and/or seeking to settle scores with the Tutsi. This wholesale, labor-intensive mass killing was in large part, carried out, using ". . .some

AK-47 assault rifles, a lot of grenades and the all-purpose slashing knives or machetes, called 'panga'. . . ."[47] Mass killing was normalized throughout Rwanda, an activity in which ". . . some local people would work 'part-time' as Interahamwe, either for the sake of looting the victim's houses, or on the contrary, to be seen as 'one of the boys' and be able to protect their own against looters." [48] Even on the local level, the Rwandan state was represented in the form of the Gendarmerie, the local and rural police. The Gendarmerie worked in tandem with the bourgmestre who "simply called on the next Gendarmerie unit and they fanned out . . . shooting and flushing people out of their homes." [49]

The state-society collaboration in mass murder was such that the Gendarmes would enlist the support of Hutu volunteers. The geographic proximity within which the Tutsi and Hutu lived helps explain the relative ease with which the killers captured and murdered very quickly so many victims. Once begun, a genocide is so difficult to halt, given that state and society are so focused on mass killing, released from any possible legal restraints. This helps explain why the mass killing took on such an extreme and sadistic tendency: "The killings were not in any way clean or surgical. The use of machetes often resulted in a long and painful agency and many people, when they had some money, paid the killers to be finished off quickly with a bullet rather than being slowly hacked to death with a panga."[50]

The enormous frenzy of mass murder even overshadows for a short period of time the scale of killing of the Holocaust.

> The hurricane of death had crushed 80 per cent of its victims in about six weeks between the second week of April and third week of May. If we consider that probably around 800,000 people were slaughtered during that short period, the daily killing rate was at least five times that of the Nazi death camps.[51]

In the end, the twisted vision of a Tutsi-free Rwanda became the manifestation of a state and society that regarded mass killing as the means with which to achieve the utopian vision of a perfect Rwanda, one of a Hutu state, capable of destroying its enemy.

Notes

1. Michael van Langenberg, "Gestapu and State Power in Indonesia" in *The Indonesian Killings of 1965-1966,* Robert Cribb, ed. (Victoria, Australia: Center of Southeast Asian Studies, Monash University, 1990) p. 47

2. *Ibid* p. 49

3. *Ibid*

4. *Ibid*

5. *Ibid* p. 52

6. *Ibid*

7. *Ibid* p. 56

8. *Ibid* p. 59

9. James Dunn, "East Timor: A Case of Cultural Genocide" in *Genocide: Conceptual and Historical Dimensions,* George Andreopoulos, ed. (Philadelphia: University of Pennsylvania Press, 1994) p. 174

10. Dunn, "Genocide in East Timor" in *Genocide in the 20th Century,* Samuel Totten, William Parsons, Israel Charny, editors (New York: Garland Publishing, 1995) p. 344

11. *Ibid*

12. Dunn, p. 345

13. James Dunn in Andreopoulos, ed., p. 184

14. Ben Kiernan, *The Pol Pot Regime* (New Haven: Yale University Press, 1996) p. 55

15. Kiernan, "The Cambodian Genocide" in *Genocide in the 20th Century,* Totten, Parsons, Charny, eds. (New York: Garland Publishing, 1995) p. 435

16. *Ibid* p. 433

17. Ervin Staub, *Roots of Evil: The Origins of Genocide and Other Group Violence* (UK: Cambridge University Press, 1989) p. 192

18. Kiernan, "The Cambodian Genocide" in *Genocide in the 20th Century* p. 437

19. *Ibid*

20. R. J. Rummel, *Death by Government* (New Jersey: Transaction Press, 1995) p. 186

21. Rummel, p. 90

22. Mahmood Mamdani, *When Victims Become Killers: Colonialism, Nativism and Genocide in Rwanda* (Princeton: Princeton University Press, 2001, p. 80)

23. Gerold Prunier, *The Rwanda Crisis: History of a Genocide* (New York: Columbia University Press, 1995) p. 49

24. Mamdani, p. 24

25. *Ibid* p. 127

26. *Ibid* p. 130

27. *Ibid* p. 129

28. *Ibid* p. 134

29. Prunier, p. 75

30. *Ibid* p. 82

31. *Ibid*
32. *Ibid* pp. 109-110
33. Prunier, p. 110
34. Prunier, pp. 137-138
35. Prunier, p. 139
36. Mamdani, p. 159
37. Prunier, p. 142
38. Mamdani, p. 210
39. *Ibid* pp. 210-211
40. Mamdani, p. 206
41. *Ibid*
42. Prunier, p. 223
43. *Ibid* p. 224
44. Prunier, p. 240
45. *Ibid* pp. 240-241
46. *Ibid* p. 244
47. Prunier, p. 243
48. *Ibid*
49. *Ibid* p. 246
50. Prunier, p. 225
51. Prunier, p. 261

Chapter 6
The Reproduction of Violence and the Pre-Genocidal State

Violence is essential to the formation of the state. Its reproduction is through the construction of a legal framework, a set of rules, which dictate how the state is permitted to express violence. So what will distinguish a pre-genocidal nation from a genocidal nation is often the quantity of violence employed by the state. But in terms of the volume of violence used, there is a thin line separating the pre-genocidal from the genocidal nation. For what makes a nation genocidal is its manifestation of an extraordinary amount of violence directed toward an identified group of victims. What sparks the transition in many cases, is some form of crisis, internal and/or external, making for a structural transformation into a dual state. The prevalance of genocide amounts to a predisposition to violence in pre-genocidal states and societies. That predisposition appears as states manufacture an ideology of violence. It is an ideology that creates a "normalization of violence." The legal promotion and regulation of violence eventually translates into making violence a functioning part of everyday life to such an extent that people even embrace violence and domesticate it. In all its many manifestations, violence is a core element of state ideology, serving to make mass violence the means of socializing a majority to live in a culture of violence. In so doing, this violent way of life in pre-genocidal societies socializes the majority to become bystanders during the transition to a genocide.

The socialization of the bystander begins in the pre-genocidal stage with the positive acceptance of violence. With this positive embrace of violence as a way of life, we have the prerequisite of bystanders, the social psychology that seeks to escape from looking at what a culture of violence implies. This has many aspects, such as the breakdown of empathy, leading to the desire to see others hurt. Ultimately, this social psychology constructs an admiration of power, which in the case of the bystander, allows submission to those in authority. To create a culture of violence is to remove any questioning of authority, upon which the power of the state rests.

The forms of violence all too common in pre-genocidal societies provide the capacity for that society to become genocidal. To the extent that "ordinary violence" is so woven into the social fabric, the majority tends to display a kind of "social numbing," that is, having no feeling for the violence all around them. The social numbing allows the majority to go about daily tasks, ignoring the violence. On one level, this is an obvious coping strategy, a recognition that it exists, but an acknowledgement on another level that it is best not to confront this violence. These aspects exist at the social level and are part of the national setting for the expression of violence. At the apex, the state, there are a number of state behaviors that predispose a nation to become genocidal. War has, for centuries, been so much a part of state policy. It has been associated with genocide but the notion of the military in partnership with state and corporate interests creates in and of itself a genocidal capacity. It is not just warmaking prior to the unfolding of a genocide, it is the preparation to wage war, which amounts to the normalization of violence. The acceptance that an arms race and the threat to use nuclear weapons are part of a culture of violence is created and recreated by state ideology. In and of itself, the idea that governments have the ability to use various weapons to quickly kill millions makes for a combination of denial and passivity by the majority. It may be a passive acceptance, but nonetheless, by and large, there is an overall refusal to confront what mass destruction means.

Besides the non-genocidal warmaking and threat of war as normalized state functions, the state produces a unique form of violence, its brand of state terrorism. With state terrorism, the state uses various forms of measured violence to send messages of intimidation, creating mass fear. What is relevant are the targets of state terrorism, all too often unarmed civilians, which illustrates the socializing effect of violence as citizens learn to accept terrorist attacks. States often work in partnership to employ selected doses of violence through surrogate terrorism. By and large, terrorism of various kinds is practiced by just about every state. The cumulative effect of warmaking, threats of war, preparation for war and state terrorism is that citizens learn to accept mass violence from the state. The majority goes about their everyday lives, accepting the presence of state violence.

States have other means of promoting violence. As long as there have been states, in varying degrees, there have been prisons, the symbolic and concrete representations of state power. To understand the function of prisons, as related to state power, is to understand how the state justifies legalized force and violence against those who employ violence for private ends. Prisons have functioned to segregate those persons regarded as undermining the social order. They have also operated as a way to implement by means of physical confinement groups that in terms of race or class have been stigmatized. Once again, with prisons, we have the extension of state power as the legal means to take physical control of a group by force. If there is a pattern of social acceptance of state power using violence, it is the support given to the prison system and its expansion against identified criminal elements.

It is no coincidence that in pre-genocidal societies, the coercive arms of the state, the military and the police are so often described in positive terms by state ideology. While at times, there may be a questioning of specific actions taken by the military and the police, there are never questions raised as to whether or not they have the right to use violence. It is also no coincidence that when genocides unfold, front and center are the military and the police as key perpetrators. This means that all nations are pre-genocidal in that they contain the potential to become genocidal, because of the creation and recreation of institutional violence inspired by fear and hatred.

Support for the state's use of normalized violence appears on the societal level as mass mobilization to manufacture an enthusiasm for organized violence and a numbness to it in the form of sports. Besides warfare, sports are a key setting for wholesale aggression and violence. With sports, we have an example of how violence is domesticated. Sports events function to make violence a recreational activity, enjoyed in one's home or at the sporting event. With sports, the state can produce cultural support for the legitimization of violence. Sports work to suspend rational thought as to the effects of violence. To view a sporting event through the technological distance of a television, the event takes on a cartoon-like quality as to the nature of the violence. It is as if no one is feeling any pain. The connections sports have in history are related to warfare. In many ways, sports imitate warfare in the manner of play, the overall goals and even the language used to describe them. Rules are in place that define the level of aggression and violence permitted. Sports permit the expression of aggression and violence within well-defined territorial boundaries against the opposition. Questions of when and how to employ force are often shaped by the fighting skills of the players, what is at stake in terms of the score and the time element. All the force used during the sport is planned well in advance with adjustments made during the course of the event. The win or the conquest of the opposition is the ultimate goal of a sport. This aspect is prevalent in contact sports, where ". . . there is every opportunity to dominate and exploit the weakness of opposing teams, allowing the victors to experience pride and the vanquished to feel humiliated."[1] If there is an ideology of sport, it is similar to state ideology in that violence and force are sanctioned as a right to use violence to exercise control and dominate others. The coach, like a head of state, is the leader authorized to mobilize the players and train them how to use violence. The players in many ways act with the discipline of a military force trained for a mission to conquer the enemy by winning. The contribution of the crowd at the sporting event takes on an atmosphere of rational suspension similar to the patriotism associated when nations wage war. There is only the final goal of winning by the violent conquest of the opposing side. To dominate is to win. To win is to use the most violence within the regulations.

It is no coincidence that the origin of sports appears in those nations associated with genocidal practices in the ancient world, Greece and Rome. The Greeks as the civilization responsible for the first organized sporting events are also credited with ". . . the vicious potential in bare-handed combat sports."[2] The Greeks originated a combination of boxing and wrestling in which "opponents fought with every part of their bodies and were free to kick, trample and use strangleholds; they could legally dislocate and break the bones of opponents."[3]

Ancient Rome had a fixation with the gladiatorial games. The power of the Roman state, associated with ongoing conquest and often mass killing had its cultural underpinnings in the Colosseum. There can be no doubt that the popular appeal of the Games was wholesale killing, which masqueraded as sport. The games were enormously popular in Rome and in the conquered territories: "Half the capital's population would pack the Colosseum at any one time, which they did with grim regularity. Throughout the empire, every provincial outpost of any consequence was able to boast its own amphitheater."[4] If there is an historic trend, it is the persistence of violent sports in which brutality and killing are only limited by the imagination of those responsible for these practices. The slaughter of not just people, but also animals continued long after the collapse of the Roman Empire. In Medieval England, it was accepted practice to arrange for animal fights:

> The tormenting of chained bears, running bulls and even monkeys, donkeys and rats with yapping, biting dogs was a staple of nearly every medieval country fair. Usually, a pack of four or five dogs was unleashed on a single bear, chained with its back to the wall. Typically, the first of the attackers were ripped to pieces within minutes, but the fight went on until the bear proved its mastery of the others or its own wounds were too severe for it to continue.[5]

This kind of social numbing to violence and killing has been the chief characteristic of so many spectator sports. Numbing is only the initial response to early exposure to violent sports. Repeated exposure produces in the minds of the viewers an actual enjoyment or pleasure in the pain and suffering of others as well as animals. This response appears in sporting events involving animals and birds,

... cockfighting, dog fighting, the bull fight have survived unchanged for almost three millennia. Today, they are still very much in evidence. In many eastern and Latin countries, fighting cocks is more popular than spending a night at the movies; throughout Spain and South America, the matador is still the modern folk hero; and in the United States. . . Sunday afternoon for hundreds of thousands of people means dying chickens, mutilated dogs and pools of blood on packed-dirt floors.[6]

As for human to human blood sports, boxing dates back to the ancient Greeks. As an Olympic sport first played in 688 B.C., it has a long and violent history. From bare-knuckle fights to later modifications, such as the introduction of padded gloves, rounds and referees, boxing retains the general idea of a violent fight in which the idea is to physically break down and destroy one's opponent.

The game as it is, has always been a contest in which two men climb into a restricted area and try to ensure that only one climbs out. The object of the game is still to purposely knock an opponent senseless. Its side products are the cut eye, the broken nose, the cracked rib, the blood in the urine, the detached retina. Its piece de resistance is the punch, which accelerates at sixty times the force of gravity to land at a speed of 30 mph with full body weight behind it.[7]

An example of group sport violence takes us to the popular sport of football, in which groups of players are on a collision course in which players of extreme weight and physical strength smash each other to the ground. The normalization of violence is characterized by the acceptance of a host of injuries. Football provides the players with a license to physically assault each other in ways very similar to a bar-room brawl. With football as with organized sports in general, what we have is state support for the legal expression of violence, which is so much a part of the culture that the majority supports the violence as acceptable behavior.

The conclusion to be reached is of sports existing as a vital, violent part of pre-genocidal nations, which function to condition a majority that violence is socially permissible:

Only sport offers the opportunity of breaking a stranger's nose, destroying another man's knee ligaments or crushing an opponent against the boards without the threat of being thrown into prison as a homicidal maniac. Only sport offers the chance of taking a life solely for the pleasure of taking life and being admired for it. Only sports offers the spectacle of all this and more for the price of a cheap ticket.Sport has it all: pain and injury, death and destruction, blood and guts, in ever-increasing doses.[8]

With state-society promoting normalized violent activities, there is a corresponding devaluation of not only human but also animal life. Such is the case with the acceptance of hunting. If there is a social psychology to mass killing during the unfolding of genocides, it is that mass killing is a learned behavior, a socialization process that begins in pre-genocidal nations as the legal license to kill beings regarded as lower forms of life. This is what we have with hunting, a social psychology driven by a will to dominate and destroy. The hunter is motivated to hunt because of the pleasure derived from killing. Killing for pleasure is also what motivates perpetrators of genocide.

It is significant that the social origins of hunting as a so-called sport is government-sponsored. With the Egyptian pharoahs, hunting was used to amuse the ruler, as was the case with the Assyrians. From the Egyptians to the Assyrians and then the Romans, the spirit of hunting takes on a territorial dimension. Rulers wanted to hunt and kill within a fixed territory. If there is an emerging pattern most striking with the Romans, hunting was a symbol of the ruler's power, useful in training for the killing during battle. The interest in hunting and killing such a large variety of animals indicates the enjoyment derived from this activity. Hunting as a ruler's prerogative continues in England during the reign of William the Conqueror, the start of the period of "royal hunts." That any animal was fair game points to hunting as being motivated by the pleasure derived from killing. The spectacle of hunting and killing large numbers of animals was over time, extended to other members of the aristocracy. By the era of the Tudors, hunts were better organized following set rituals.

> Each different species was dispatched and dissected in accordance with its own set of rules. . ..Harts, for example, were ceremonially run through with swords by the hunters who would then dip bread in the gore to be fed to the hounds. The various parts of the carcass were removed and awarded to selected hunters and onlookers. Blood, in particular, held an almost mystical fascination and was liberally smeared over all present. . .[9]

In one regard, the hunting and killing of animals is the power of the ruler having without thought and much delight the right to destroy lesser beings. It is also about making hunting a "normal" function of the ruler, although what was deemed a normal activity for a head of state was in practice a perverse, sadistic practice, especially during the rule of Louis XIV in France. Louis XIV, a hunting enthusiast,

> . . . invented La Curee (the Kill), a strange and sordid pageant which was performed whenever an animal was cornered. When the hunting horns trumpeted a special fanfare, the lead dog was encouraged to sink its teeth into the animal's

skull. Then the rest of the pack was loosed to tear out its entrails.[10]

The extension of hunting as a democratic pastime happened with the invention of the gun. From this moment, the hunting and killing of animals on a global scale was without historical precedent. The gun and a legal license to shoot and kill makes violence and killing domestic, a normal source of entertainment. The psychology of hunting and the killing as the end product, functions in accordance with the construction of rationalizations, as a division of human and non-human. Human selfhood emerges in sharp contrast to the non-human other. In America, even the Puritans, who prided themselves as being so moral participated in "cooperative hunts, such as the wolf drives on mid-winter Sundays after Church became the closest thing to a public holiday the Puritans allowed themselves."[11] By making the distinction between self and other, any inhibitions about killing are removed. Large-scale hunting becomes an exercise of removal, taking away what offends us. How else can we explain such actions as the wholesale slaughter of the buffalo in the United States?

Instilling destructive impulses serves a functional purpose for states, as a part of military training. Such is the case for officers in the Army of India.

> For the officers of the Imperial forces, *shikar* was all but a duty. In the eyes of the high command, good hunters made good officers. Leave was invariably a carefully planned two-month expedition to the teak forests of the interior after elephant, tiger, panther, cheetah, bear, boar and bison. . . or to the Ganges Delta for rhinoceros, buffalo and big cats. [12]

The otherness of animals unleashes a willingness to engage in the wholesale destruction of entire species. In South Africa, the interior colonization of the country brought with it during the "Great Trek," the near extinction of many species. "Within forty years of the start of the Great Trek, most of Southern Africa had been denuded of its big game."[13] What we have is this social psychology in many pre-genocidal nations, in which killing that which is different is an accepted social practice. It is not a coincidence that those defined as different have been targeted for mass killing. It is also no coincidence that the psychology of hunting contains coded language so as not to use the word 'kill.' What we have are words such as ". . . 'culled,' 'harvested,' 'reduced,' 'cropped' or 'controlled.'"[14]

Another example of ordinary violence producing social numbing to mass killing in pre-genocidal nations, is the industry of death responsible for turning animals into food for humans to consume. The essence of this process is the manner in which animals are transformed from living beings into commodities through an assembly line of death in the slaughterhouse.

It was in the Chicago meat packing industry that we have the inventors Gustavius Swift and Philip Armour, who created the assembly line model for killing animals, which in turn, inspired Henry Ford and later, the Nazis. The mass killing of animals follows a standardized procedure:

> The steers enter the slaughterhouse single file. Immediately upon entry, they are stunned by a pneumatic gun. As each animal sinks to its knees, a worker quickly hooks a chain onto a rear hoof and the animal is mechanically hoisted from the platform and hung upside down over the slaughterhouse floor. Men in blood-soaked gowns, handling long knives slit each steer's threat, thrusting the blade deep into the larynx for a second or two, then quickly withdrawing the knife, severing the jugular vein and carotid artery in the process. Blood spurts out over the workstation, splattering the workers and the equipment. The dead animal moves along the main disassembly line. At the next workstation, the animal is skinned. The hide is cut open at the midline of the stomach and a skinning machine strips the animal of its hide, leaving the skin in one piece. The carcass is decapitated, the tongue is split and removed and both head and tongue are impaled on hooks attached to the disassembly line chain. The carcass is then gutted. The liver, heart, intestines and other organs are removed. After the viscera are removed, the body is hurried along to the next station, where the carcass is cut down the center of the backbone with motorized saws and the tail is pulled off the animal. The split carcass is hosed down with warm water, wrapped in cloth and sent to a meat cooler for twenty-four hours. The next day, workers use power saws to cut the carcass into recognizable cuts: steaks, chuck, ribs, brisket.[15]

It is this acceptance of assembly line killing of animals as 'normal' that places a distance between what happens to them and us. The idea of killing from a distance, a trait found in many genocides, first appears in pre-genocidal societies as a way of not confronting what is done to these animals, ". . . cattle and other livestock are tucked away, out of sight of the public, until they are purchased in the form of prepacked cuts of beef at the local supermarket."[16] The killing is also rationalized by the utility of the animals made into so many products sold to consumers:

> More than 40 per cent of the animal—fat, bones, viscera, hide—is converted by renderers into a range of substances, materials and products used in the preparation of other foods, household products, pharmaceuticals and industrial products. [17]

All too common in so many genocides is the use of animal metaphors. The dehumanization of humans follows the denial of a right to life to animals. In this denial, dehumanized humans are slaughtered like animals. For one Holocaust survivor, the assembly line killing of animals came to resemble the same process applied to people. In ". . . the slaughterhouse, like aspects of the Holocaust, she started to understand the connection between the industrialized slaughter of animals and the industrialized slaughter of people."[18] The most obvious conclusion to arrive at, given this industrial slaughter of animals, is that they have no right to exist, other than to satisfy our cultivated preference to consume the flesh of animals and their remaining parts as consumer goods. While animals cannot directly communicate a right to exist except when they are at the door of the slaughterhouse, human beings do communicate to each other when they are in the process of giving up their rights.

In pre-genocidal societies, human beings give up their freedom to be free from violence. Instead, the arbitrary use of force is embraced. The majority who will eventually become the bystanders during a genocide have accepted violence as a way of life. In so doing, the state can enforce in ever-increasing doses the use of violence as a means of social control. What is a pattern in modern genocides is the increasing spread of violence as a positive value with the state increasing control to the point of forming a police state. With pre-modern genocides, state power functioned without popular support. The sovereignty of the state meant it had absolute authority to act in the formulation of policy. In essence, police power was the manifestation of the state's sovereignty to carry out policies by force. Under the democratic revolutions in the Western world, in spite of those elites who were represented, the ruler was free to act without legal restraint, given the fact that the monarch defined what is legal. The monarch had the authority to act in the interests of the state and not just to further his own private interests.

With the appearance of the first type of police state or Polizeistatt comes the idea that the state should have both the supreme authority and power to act without restraint to maintain social order. With this notion, the state acquires total control over social activities. This social control was intended to promote the virtuous actions of the state. So the exercise of total control over society was tempered by rules, which regulated state action. What this also implies, is if the state perceives a serious threat to social order, its ability to act is unimpaired by any legal stipulations. In addition, actions which further state interests allow for the Polizeistatt without any limitations. As was so often the case, pre-modern genocides unfolded when states exercised police power using extreme violence to claim a monopoly of force as the state seized new territories. The result was all too often an effort to destroy people who stood in the way of this goal. So when the state is the final judge of threats to order, it can act without legal limits. In essence, the modern police states acted as political police. Such was the case with Joseph II of Prussia and Fouche of France, who set up the state to monitor 'who is thinking what' and if these thoughts are a threat to the state. In these police states, the state gathers intelligence by organizing and centralizing control over society for the good of society. State repression of a threat is the end result of this paternalism. What is significant is that the political police operate as a specialized branch of state power. Over time, police powers were evolving, becoming not only a national police but also one which was decentralized so as to function as a local police force.

While the pre-modern police states acted to protect the state from threats, the modern police state has as its goal the political indoctrination of the people. The modern police state with Nazi Germany as the classic example made the Fuhrer Hitler the absolute ruler because his power was derived from the Constitution. This manufacture of legal authority was supplemented by his position as the representative of the German people. With the transformation of the German police in the 1930s, which was completed in 1939 with the Reich Main Security Headquarters, the modern police state is born. With ideology and coercion blended into an independent state structure, Germany created the structural prerequisite for mass murder. In effect, anti-Semitic ideology and violence from this specialized part of the German state permeated not only the German state, but all of German society.

If there is a pattern in pre-genocidal nations that creates a predisposition to become genocidal, it is the formation of a police state, which infuses ideology into police functions. The police state by virtue of it having the force to implement its ideology operates as a state within a state. It functions to exercise a forceful control over society. As a state within a state, it is free to operate without judicial or civil restraints and has its own paramilitary policing units. For its authority to reign supreme and ultimately for a police state to function, everyone inside and outside of government is a potential threat. At the same time, a modern police state is a mobilizer of people not only in terms of a steady stream of propaganda to politically reeducate but also to marshall support for the actions it takes. As it is in part a product of democracy, the modern police state mobilizes the democratic principles for anti-democratic goals. In so doing, a police state is in a perverted sense legitimized by the support given to its takeover and control of social policy, it also has encroached upon the state in general. The police state encroaches, yet remains independent from any legal controls. By and large, if there is a long term goal of a police state, it is ". . . to attempt to control every field open to infiltration."[19] The police state seeks to infiltrate the minds of the people. The police state is a particular philosophy of the state. A police state will emerge out of conditions prevalent in society and is further enhanced by those seeking to reform the state. With this in mind, one should revisit the previous discussion of how ordinary violence has made for a kind of "social numbing." If the police state is anything, it is a worship and glorification of violence. When societies foster a host of violent practices, be it militarism, violent sports or the industrial slaughter of animals, the society plants the seeds to germinate a state which settles conflict only by resorting to force. From the case studies presented, it is clear that the genocidal practices of the dual state are in many ways manifestations of a police state, which has identified an enemy and seeks to destroy it during a crisis. The police state is transformed into a dual state, genocidal in its intention, when there is an ideological shift from regarding all of society as a threat to one small segment. A crisis either internal and/or external propels that part of the state to reassert its power by an extraordinary use of its monopoly of violence.

If there is a conclusion to be reached by way of a few words on the issue of genocide prevention, it is twofold. One preventative measure is to rein in the power of the state. This would amount to a social revolution which in the end would place meaningful legal restraints on the state's use of its coercive might. It can be argued that the restraints in place are wholly inadequate. The second preventative measure is for societies to create a culture of life, one that is supportive of activities which promote non-violence.

Notes

1. John Kerr, *Rethinking Aggression in Sport* (New York: Routledge Press, 2005) p. 58

2. Robert Yeager, *Seasons of Shame* (New York: McGraw-Hill, 1979) p. 128

3. *Ibid*

4. Don Atyeo, *Blood and Guts: Violence in Sports* (New York: Paddington Press, 1979) p. 133

5. Yeager, pp. 135-135

6. Atyeo, p. 85

7. *Ibid* p. 180

8. *Ibid* p. 357

9. *Ibid* p. 27

10. *Ibid*

11. *Ibid* p. 34

12. *Ibid* pp. 45-46

13. *Ibid* p. 49

14. *Ibid* p. 71

15. Jeremy Rifkin, *Beyond Beef* (New York: Dutton Press, 1992) pp. 14-15

16. *Ibid* p. 279

17. *Ibid* p. 274

18. Charles Patterson, *Eternal Treblinka* (New York: Lantern Books, 2002) p. 49

19. Brian Chapman, *Police State* (New York: Praeger Press, 1970) p. 123

Bibliography

Alvarez, Alex. *Governments, Citizens and Genocide*. Indiana: Indiana University Press, 2001

Andreopoulos, George J. *Genocide: Conceptual and Historical Dimensions*. Philadelphia: University of Pennsylvania Press, 1994

Arad, Yitzhak. *Belzec, Sobibor, Treblinka*. Bloomington: Indiana Press, 1987

Atyeo, Don. *Blood and Guts: Violence in Sports*. New York: Paddington Press, 1979

Augenda, G. *Effects of War on Society*. New York: Boydell Press, 1992

Bramstedt, E.K. *Dictatorship and Political Police*. UK: Kegan Paul, 1945

Burleigh, Michael. *The Third Reich*. New York: Macmillan Press, 2000

Carlton, Eric. *Militarism*. Vermont: Aghate Publishing, 2001

Cesarani, David, ed. *The Final Solution*. New York: Routledge, 1994

Chalk, Frank, and Kurt Jonassohn. *The History and Sociology of Genocide*. New Haven: Yale University Press, 1990

Chapman, Brian. *Police State*. New York: Praeger Press, 1970

Claessent, Henri and Peter Skalnik, eds. *The Early State*. New York: Mouton Publishers, 1978

Cohen, Ronald, and Elman Service, eds. *Origins of the State*. Philadelphia: Institute for the Study of Human Issues, 1978

Conquest, Robert. *The Harvest of Sorrow*. New York: Oxford Press, 1986

Cribb, Robert, ed. *The Indonesian Killings of 1965-1966*. Victoria: Center of Southeast Asian Studies, Monash University, 1990

Dadrian, Vahakn N. *The History of the Armenian Genocide*. UK: Berghahn Books, 1995

Dallen, David and Boris Nicolevsky, *Forced Labor in Soviet Russia*. New Haven: Yale University Press, 1993

Doyne Dawson, *The Origins of Warfare*. UK: Harper Collins, 1996

Donat, Alexander. *The Death Camp Treblinka*. New York: Holocaust Library, 1979

Farber, Samuel. *Before Stalinism: The Rise and Fall of Soviet Democracy*. UK: Polity Press, 1990

Fraenkel, Ernst. *The Dual State*. UK: Oxford University Press, 1941

Fouret, Francois. *Unanswered Questions: Nazi Germany and the Genocide of the Jews*.

New York: Schocken Books, 1989

Frank, Hans. excerpt from Nuremberg trials transcript, governmental conference, August 24, 1942 http://www.yale.edu/lawweb/avalon/imt/proc/02-25-46.htm

Gellately, Robert and Ben Kiernan. *The Specter of Genocide: Mass Murder in Historical Perspective.* New York: Cambridge University Press, 2003

Giddens, Anthony. *The Nation State and Violence.* California: University of California Press, 1985

Gutman, Yisrael and Michael Berenbaum, eds. *Anatomy of the Auschwitz Death Camp.* Indianapolis: Indiana University Press, 1994

Hall, John, ed. *States in History.* UK: Basil Blackwell, 1986

Hinton, Alexander Laban, ed. *Annihilating Difference.* California: University of California Press, 2002

Hohne, Heinz. *The Order of the Death's Head.* New York: Ballantine Books, 1989

Holsti, Kalevi. *The State, War and the State of War.* UK: Cambridge University Press, 1996

Hovaninisian, Richard. *The Armenian Genocide in Perspective.* New Jersey: Transaction Press, 1986

Huntington, Samuel. *The Soldier and the State.* New York: Vintage Books, 1964

Jakobson, Michael. *Origins of the Gulag: the Soviet Prison Correctional System 1917-1934.* Lexington: University of Kentucky Press, 1993

Je Jasay, Anthony. *The State.* UK: Basil Blackwell, 1985

Kerr, John. *Rethinking Aggression and Violence in Sport.* New York: Routledge Press, 2005

Kiernan, Ben. *The Pol Pot Regime.* New Haven: Yale University Press, 1996

Klee, Ernst, Willie Dresser, Volker Riess. *Those Were the Days.* U.K.: Hannish Hamilton, 1991

Kogon, Eugen ed. *Nazi Mass Murder: A Documentary History of the Use of Poison Gas.* New Haven: Yale University Press, 1993

Lewin, Moshe. *The Making of the Soviet System.* New York: Norton Press, 1994

Lewin, Moshe. *Russian Peasants and Soviet Power.* Evanston: Northwestern University Press, 1968

Libaridian, Gerald. *The Armenian Genocide.* UK: The Zaryan Institute, 1985

Mamdani, Mahmood. *When Victims Become Killers.* New Jersey: Princeton University Press, 2001

Mann, Michael. *The Sources of Social Power.* UK: Cambridge University Press, 1986

Melson, Robert. *Revolution and Genocide.* Chicago: University of Chicago Press, 1992

Midlarsky, Manus. *The Killing Trap.* UK: Cambridge University Press, 2005

Piper, Franciszek. *Auschwitz 1940-1945.* (Oswiecim: Auschwitz State Museum, 2000

Porter, Bruce. *War and the Rise of the State.* New York: Free Press, 1994

Prunier, Gerald. *The Rwanda Crisis: History of a Genocide.* New York: Columbia University Press, 1995

Rifkin, Jeremy. *Beyond Beef.* New York: Dutton Press, 1992

Rubenstein, William. *Genocide.* New York: Pearsan, Longman, 2004

Rummel, R.J. *Death by Government.* New Jersey: Transaction Publishers, 1994

Shaw, Martin. *War and Genocide.* U.K.: Polity Press, 2003

Sicker, Martin. *The Genesis of the State.* New York: Praeger Press, 1991

Staub, Erwin *The Roots of Evil: The Origins of Genocide and Other Forms of Group Violence.* New York: Cambridge University Press, 1990

Suakian, Kevork. The Preconditions of the Armenian Turkish Case of Genocide in *American Review* Vol 34, 1981

Tilly, Charles. *The Formation of National States in Western Europe.* Princeton: Princeton University Press, 1975

Totten, Samuel, William Parsons and Israel W. Charny, *Genocide in the 20th Century.* New York: Garland Publishing, 1995

van den Berghe, Peter L., ed. *State Violence and Ethnicity.* Colorado: University of Colorado Press, 1990

Vogts, Alfred. *A History of Militarism.* New York: Free Press, 1967

Valentino, Benjamin. *Final Solutions: Mass Killing and Genocide in the 20th Century.* Ithaca: Cornell University Press, 2004

Wallimann, Isidor, and Michael Dobkowski, *Genocide and the Modern Age.* New York: Greenwood Press, 1987

Weitz, Eric. *A Century of Genocide.* Princeton: Princeton University Press, 2003

Williams, Robin. *The Wars Within.* New York: Cornell University Press, 2003

Yeager, Robert. *Seasons of Shame.* New York: McGraw-Hill, 1979

Index

Author Biography

Andrew Kolin, Ph.D., is a professor of law and government at Hilbert College in Hamburg, New York. He teaches courses in many subfields of political science including Genocide, The Holocaust, Gender Politics and Politics and the Media.

He is the author of *The Ethical Foundations of Hume's Theory of Politics,*"Major Concepts in Politics and Political Theory, Vol. I," (Peter Lang, 1992); and two editions of *One Family: Before and During the Holocaust,* (University Press of America) published in 2003 and 2000.

Prior to teaching at Hilbert College, Kolin was an assistant professor of political science at Waynesburg College in Waynesburg, Pennsylvania. He also has taught political science at Brooklyn College, the John Jay College of Criminal Justice, and City College in New York. He earned his doctorate from the City University of New York Graduate Center.